CATASTROPHE AND SOCIAL CHANGE

LECTOR HOUSE PUBLIC DOMAIN WORKS

CATASTROPHE AND SOCIAL CHANGE

SAMUEL HENRY PRINCE

ISBN: 978-93-5614-654-9

Published: 1920

LECTOR HOUSE

LECTOR HOUSE LLP
E-MAIL: info@lectorhouse.com

CATASTROPHE
AND
SOCIAL CHANGE

BASED UPON A SOCIOLOGICAL STUDY OF THE HALIFAX DISASTER

BY

SAMUEL HENRY PRINCE, M. A. (TOR.)

SUBMITTED IN PARTIAL FULFILMENT OF THE REQUIREMENTS
FOR THE DEGREE OF DOCTOR OF PHILOSOPHY
IN THE
FACULTY OF POLITICAL SCIENCE
COLUMBIA UNIVERSITY

1920

Halifax
is not a large city
but there are those who love it
who would choose to dwell therein
before all cities beneath
the skies

TO

ALL SUCH

CITIZENS, PAR EXCELLENCE,

I COUNT IT AN HONOR TO DEDICATE

THESE LINES

PREFACE

THE following pages embody the result of an observational study of the social phenomena attendant upon one of the greatest catastrophies in history—the Halifax Disaster. The idea of the work was suggested while carrying out a civic community study of the disaster city under the direction of Professor F. H. Giddings of Columbia University.

The account deals first with the shock and disintegration as the writer observed it. Individual and group reactions are next examined in the light of sociological theory. The chapters on Social Organization are an effort to picture that process as it actually occurred.

The writer has also tried faithfully to record any important contribution which Social Economy was able to make in the direction of systematic rehabilitation. Special reference is made to private initiative and governmental control in emergency relief. This monograph is in no sense, however, a relief survey. Its chief value to the literature of relief will lie in its bearing upon predictable social movements in great emergencies.

Nor is the book a history of the disaster. It is rather, as the title suggests, an intensive study of two social orders, between which stands a great catastrophe, and its thesis is the place of catastrophe in social change.

In the preparation of this work, which the author believes to be the first attempt to present a purely scientific and sociological treatment of any great disaster, he has received invaluable assistance. A few grateful lines can ill-express his obligation to his Professors of the Department of Sociology. To Professor F. H. Giddings the volume owes its inspiration and much of its social philosophy. To Professor A. A. Tenney it owes its present form and structure and any literary excellence it may possess. Professor R. E. Chaddock has read the manuscript throughout and has contributed many helpful suggestions. Professor S. M. Lindsay has read the chapter on Social Legislation, and Professor R. S. Woodworth of the Department of Psychology, that on Disaster Psychology. The author is under special tribute to Professor H. R. Seager, and to Professor Tenney, who most cheerfully sacrificed part of a summer vacation to read and revise the manuscript and proof.

Without the walls of the University there are also those who have given aid. The author gratefully acknowledges the assistance of Dr. Edward T. Devine of New York, of Mr. C. C. Carstens of Boston, of Mr. Thomas Mackay, of Ottawa, and of Miss E. M. A. Vaughan, of the St. John Public Library. He has enjoyed the coöperation of many friends and fellow-townsmen of Halifax. He desires to thank particularly, Miss L. F. Barnaby, of the Halifax Citizens' Library, Miss J. B. Wisdom, of the Halifax Welfare Bureau, Rev. W. J. Patton of St. Paul's Church, Mr. W. C. Milner, of the Public Archives of Canada, Mr. L. Fred. Monaghan, Halifax City Clerk, Mr. G. K. Butler, Supervisor of Halifax Schools, Mr. R. M. Hattie, Secretary of the Halifax Town-Planning Commission, Dr. Franklin B. Royer, Director of the Massachusetts-Halifax Health Commission, Mr. E. A. Saunders, Secretary of the Halifax Board of Trade, Mr. E. H. Blois, Superintendent of Neglected and Delinquent Children, and last of all and most of all his friend of many years, Mr. A. J. Johnstone, editor of the *Dartmouth Independent*.

S. H. P.

Columbia University, New York, October, 1920.

CONTENTS

Page

Preface vi

INTRODUCTION

- The "catastrophe" in sociological literature xiv
- The "catastrophic view" vs. progress in evolution xiv
- Factors in social change xv
- The stimuli factors xv
- What crises mean. xvi
- Communities and great vicissitudes xvii
- Causes of immobility. xviii
- Catastrophe and progress xix
- Historic cases suggested for study xix

CHAPTER I

CATASTROPHE AND SOCIAL DISINTEGRATION

- The City of Halifax 1
- Terrific nature of the explosion 1
- Destruction of life and property 2
- The subsequent fire and storms. 3
- Annihilation of homes 4
- Arresting of business. 4
- Disintegration of the social order 5

CHAPTER II

CATASTROPHE AND SOCIAL PSYCHOLOGY

- Shock reaction 7
- Hallucination 8
- Primitive instincts 9
- Crowd psychology 10
- Phenomena of emotion 12
- How men react when bereft completely 14
- Post-catastrophic phenomena 15
- Human nature in the absence of repression by conventionality, custom and law 15
- Fatigue and the human will 17
- The stimuli of heroism 18
- Mutual aid 19

CHAPTER III

CATASTROPHE AND SOCIAL ORGANIZATION

- The organization of relief 21
- The disaster protocracy 22
- The transition from chaos through leadership 22
- Utility of association 22
- Vital place of communication 22
- Imitation 23
- Social pressure 23
- Consciousness of kind 23
- Discussion 24
- Circumstantial pressure 24
- Climate 24
- Geographic determinants 25
- Classification of factors 25

CHAPTER IV

CATASTROPHE AND SOCIAL ORGANIZATION (CONT'D)

- The reorganization of the civil social order 27
- Division of labor 27
- Resumption of normal activities 28

- State and voluntary associations 28
- Order of reëstablishment 28
- Effects of environmental change 31
- The play of imitation 32
- The stimulus of lookers-on 32
- Social conservation 33

CHAPTER V

CATASTROPHE AND SOCIAL ECONOMY

- The contribution of social service 34
- Its four-fold character 36
- The principles of relief 37
- Rehabilitation 38
- Phases of application 38
- Criticisms 41
- A new principle 43
- Social results 43
- Summary for future guidance 44

CHAPTER VI

CATASTROPHE AND SOCIAL LEGISLATION

- Governmental agencies in catastrophe 47
- What seems to be expected of governments 47
- What they actually do 47
- Social legislation 48
- A permanent contribution 51

CHAPTER VII

CATASTROPHE AND SOCIAL SURPLUS

- Mill's explanation of the rapidity with which communities recover from disaster 53
- The case of San Francisco 53
- The case of Halifax 53
- Social surplus 53
- The equipmental factors 54

- Correlation of tragedy in catastrophe with generosity of public response. . 54
- Catastrophe insurance 56
- A practical step 56

CHAPTER VIII

CATASTROPHE AND SOCIAL CHANGE

- The unchanging Halifax of the years. 57
- The causes of social immobility. 57
- The new birthday. 59
- The indications of change—appearance, expansion of business, population, political action, city-planning, housing, health, education, recreation, community spirit 60
- Carsten's prophecy. 70

CHAPTER IX

CONCLUSION

- Recapitulation. 72
- The various steps in the study presented in propositional form 72
- The rôle of catastrophe. 74

Index. 77

"This awful catastrophe is not the end but the beginning. History does not end so. It is the way its chapters open." —*St. Augustine.*

INTRODUCTION

The "catastrophe" in sociological literature—The "catastrophic view" *vs.* progress in evolution—Factors in social change—The stimuli factors—What crises mean—Communities and great vicissitudes—Causes of immobility—Catastrophe and progress—Historic cases suggested for study.

There are many virgin fields in Sociology. This is one of the attractions the subject has for the scientific mind. But of all such fields none is more interesting than the factor of catastrophe in social change.

And strangely enough, if there are but few references to the problem in all our rapidly-growing literature, it is not because catastrophies are few. Indeed it would seem that with the advent of the industrial age, disasters grow more frequent every year.[1] Many are small, no doubt, touching but the life of a village or a borough—a broken dyke, a bridge swept out by ice, a caved-in mine. Others again write themselves on the pages of History—an Ohio flood, an Omaha tornado, a Chicago fire, a San Francisco earthquake, a Halifax explosion. Each in its own way inscribes its records of social change—some to be effaced in a twelve-month—some to outlast a generation. Records they are, for the most part unread. How to read them is the problem. And it may be that when readers have grown in number and the script is better known, we shall be able to seize the moment of catastrophe and multiply immeasurably its power for social good.

To define the term catastrophe is scarcely necessary. The dictionary calls catastrophe "an event producing a subversion of the order or system of things," and such as "may or may not be a cause of misery to man."[2] It is desirable however to limit the use of the term, in primary investigations at least, to those disasters which affect communities rather than states or nations, for restricted areas are more amenable to study. National cataclysms, such as war, famine, and financial panic are too general in character, and function on too grand a scale for satisfactory treatment, at least until the ground is cleared. It is necessary also to limit this investigation to those social changes which follow upon catastrophies, rather than

[1] "Within a score of years disasters ... have cost thousands of lives, have affected by personal injury, or destruction of property no fewer than a million and a half persons and have laid waste property valued at over a billion dollars ... the expectation based on past experience is that each year no less than half a dozen such catastrophies will occur." (Deacon J. Byron, *Disasters*, N. Y., 1918, p. 7.) This quotation refers to the United States alone.

[2] Catastrophies are those unforeseen events which the Wells-Fargo express receipts used to call quaintly "Acts of God, Indians and other public enemies of the government."

precede them. For there are social effects which result from living in anticipation of disaster, such as are observable among communities in volcanic areas. Interesting as a broad study might be, it would be likely to lead the investigator too far afield into the realm of speculation. Nevertheless a general point of view is necessary to give meaning to even a limited treatment of the theme. For this purpose there may be contrasted the catastrophic view of history, as illustrated by that of the Hebrew peoples, and the modern conception of progress through evolution. The former looks upon history as a series of vicissitudes mercifully ending one day in final cataclysm. The spirit of apocalyptic expectancy prevails. Social conditions rest hopelessly static. Faith is pinned to a spiritual kingdom which can grow and can endure. Against this has been set an optimistic evolution, pictured like an escalade with resident forces lifting the world to better days. Progress becomes a smooth continuous growth. On the other hand the newer philosophy sees in history not necessarily the operation of progressive evolution but also of retrogressive evolution and cataclysm.[3] There are great stretches of smooth and even current in the stream, but always along the course are seen the rapid and the water-fall, the eddy and reversing tide. The latter is the general subject of this dissertation, and its thesis is the place of the water-fall. Only a very small, and specialized treatment is attempted; the great Niagaras must be left to abler hands.

The conception of social change as used in this monograph also needs definition. By social change is meant those rapid mutations which accompany sudden interferences with the equilibrium of society, break up the *status-quo,* dissipate mental inertia and overturn other tendencies resistant to structural modification. The various forces which initiate such disturbances are factors in social change. These factors may be intra-social,—within the group—such factors as operate in the regular social process, imitation and adaptation, for example; or they may be extra-social, "stimuli" factors—from without the group—such as, accidental, extraneous or dramatic events. Of the latter conquest may be one, or the sudden intrusion of a foreign element, or rapid changes of environment.[4]

These sudden changes are fully worthy of careful study by scientific method. However important the accumulation of impulses toward social transformation may be, there is often a single "precipitating factor" which acts as the "igniting spark" or "the knocking away of the stay-block," or "the turning of a lever."[5] It is among such extra-social or "stimuli" factors that catastrophe falls as a precipitating agent in social change.

[3] If nature abhors a vacuum, she also abhors stagnation. Is there not reason behind all this action and reaction, these cycles and short-time changes which her observers note? May it not well be that the ever-swinging pendulum has a stir-up function to perform and that the miniature daily catastrophies of life are the things which keep it wholesome and sweet?

> "The old order changeth yielding place to the new.
> And God fulfils Himself in many ways
> Lest one good custom should corrupt the world."
>
> —Tennyson, Alfred, *The Passing of Arthur.*

[4] Ross, Edward A., *Foundations of Sociology* (N. Y., 1905), ch. viii, p. 189.

[5] Ross, *op. cit.,* p. 198.

The significance of crisis in social change likewise requires attention, and it will be clarifying to our thought at this point to distinguish carefully between crisis and catastrophe, and to inquire what the nature of the former really is. The word "crisis" is of Greek origin, meaning a point of culmination and separation, an instant when change one way or another is impending. Crises are those critical moments which are, as we say, big with destiny. Battles have crisis-hours when the tide of victory turns. Diseases have them—the seventh day in pneumonia, or the fourteenth day in typhoid fever. Social institutions afford numerous illustrations, such as the eighth year of marriage.[6] There are critical years of stress and strain—the ages of fourteen and forty in life-histories, the latter being according to Sir Robertson Nicoll the most dangerous hour of existence. Other crises are "hours of insight" in the world of thought, and hours of opportunity in the world of action,—that "tide in the affairs of men, which taken at the flood leads on to fortune," hours of doubt in religion "when all the gods are dead." "Crisis," Professor Shailer Mathews observes, "is something more than a relative term. It describes a situation which is no ordinary member of a line of antecedents and consequents, but one that assures radical change in the immediate future." He distinguishes between a crisis and a revolution. "The difference between a revolution and a crisis is the difference between the fire and the moment when someone with a lighted match in hand pauses to decide whether a fire shall be lighted." The term covers the situation preceding change, whether this situation be the culmination of a process or the result of some particular stimulus. "It is not necessarily precipitated by great issues. Quite as often it is occasioned by events .... which are so related to a new situation as to set in motion an entire group of forces as a match kindles a huge bonfire when once the fuel is laid."[7] The failure to distinguish between that which occasions the crisis and the crisis itself has been the source of some confusion in thinking. "Defeat in battle, floods, drought, pestilence and famine," are not strictly crises, but they super-induce the crisis-situation, as does anything which brings about "a disturbance of habit," though it be simply "an incident, a stimulation or a suggestion." In short, crises are the result either of a slowly maturing process or of sudden strain or shock; and the nature of the reaction in the crisis-hour is nothing more than the effort towards the reëstablishment of habits, new or old, when the former functioning has been disturbed. The situation, as has been pointed out, is closely correlated with attention.

> When the habits are running smoothly the attention is relaxed; it is not at work. But when something happens to disturb the run of habit, the attention is called into play, and devises a new mode of behavior which will meet the crisis. That is, the attention establishes new and adequate habits, or it is its function so to do.[8]

What appears to take place is analogous to what is known as the reconditioning of instincts in psychology. Professor Giddings has been the first to make the sociological application:

[6] Jeune, Sir Francis, a celebrated judge in divorce cases.

[7] Mathews, Shailer, *The Church in the Changing Order* (N. Y., 1907), ch. i, p. 1.

[8] Thomas, William I., *Source Book of Social Origins* (Chicago, 1909), Introduction, p. 17.

> Folk-ways of every kind, including mores and themistes are the most stable syntheses of pluralistic behavior; yet they are not unchanging. Under new and widening experience they suffer attrition and are modified. Instincts and with them emotion and imagination which largely fills the vast realm between instinct and reason are reconditioned. The word means simply that reflexes and higher processes subjected to new experiences are in a degree or entirely detached from old stimuli and associated with new ones. From time to time also traditions are invaded and habits are broken down by crisis. Pluralistic behavior then is scrutinized, criticized, discussed. It is rationally deliberated.[9]

Crises often, perhaps most often, precede catastrophies, as when revolutions break. The alternate truth that the catastrophies themselves are re-agents to generate the crisis-situation has not been so commonly noted. Nevertheless the disintegration of the normal by shock and calamity is an increasingly familiar spectacle.

Heretofore it has been in the life-histories and careers of individual men rather than in the case of communities that the observations have been recorded. Our biographies teem with instances of personal crises precipitated by a great shock or disappointment—Hawthorne's dismissal from the custom house, Goldsmith's rejection from Civil Service, the refusal of Dickens's application for the stage, the turning back of Livingstone from China, the bankruptcy of Scott.

Now examination reveals that the one thing characteristic of the crisis-period in the individual is a state of fluidity[10] into which the individual is thrown. Life becomes like molten metal. It enters a state of flux[11] from which it must reset upon a principle, a creed, or purpose. It is shaken perhaps violently out of rut and routine. Old customs crumble, and instability rules. There is generated a state of potentiality for reverse directions. The subject may "fall down" or he may "fall up." The presence of dynamic forces in such a state means change. But the precise rôle of the individual mind in a period of crisis is a problem not for sociology but for psychology.

The principle that fluidity is fundamental to social change is also true, however, of the community. Fluidity is not the usual state of society.

> Most of the "functions" of society have no tendency to disturb the *status quo*. The round of love, marriage and reproduc-

[9] Giddings, Franklin H., "Pluralistic Behaviour," *American Journal of Sociology*, vol. xxv, no. 4 (Jan., 1920), p. 401.

[10] The phrases "The world in a welter," "nations in the melting pot," "life in the smelting oven," are commonly heard and suggest a solution stage prior to the hardening process, or antecedent to crystallization.

[11] Following the French Revolution Wordsworth wrote:

> I lost
> All feeling of conviction and in fine
> Sick, wearied out with contrarieties
> Yielded up moral questions in despair.
>
> —*Prelude*, bk. xi.

> tion, so long as births and death balance, production so far as it is balanced by consumption, exchange so long as the argosies of commerce carry goods and not ideas, education so far as it passes on the traditional culture, these together with recreation, social intercourse, worship, social control, government and the administration of justice are essentially statical. They might conceivably go on forever without producing change.[12]

Indeed the usual condition of the body politic is immobility, conservatism and "determined resistance to change." The chief reason for this immobility is habit:[13]

> When our habits are settled and running smoothly they most resemble the instincts of animals. And the great part of our life is lived in the region of habit. The habits like the instincts are safe and serviceable. They have been tried and are associated with a feeling of security. There consequently grows up in the folk mind a determined resistance to change ... a state of rapid and constant change implies loss of settled habits and disorganization. As a result, all societies view change with suspicion, and the attempt to revise certain habits is even viewed as immorality. Now it is possible under such conditions for a society to become stationary or to attempt to remain so. The effort of attention is to preserve the present status, rather than to re-accommodate. This condition is particularly marked among savages. In the absence of science and a proper estimate of the value of change they rely on ritual and magic and a minute unquestioning adhesion to the past. Change is consequently introduced with a maximum of resistance ... Indeed the only world in which change is at a premium and is systematically sought is the modern scientific world.[14]

But when there comes the shattering of the matrix of custom by catastrophe, then mores are broken up and scattered right and left. Fluidity is accomplished at a stroke. There comes a sudden chance for permanent social change.

Social changes follow both minor and major disasters. The destruction of a mill may change the economic outlook of a village. The loss of a bridge may result in an entirely different school system for an isolated community; a cloud-burst may move a town. Great visitations, like the Chicago fire or the San Francisco earthquake, reveal these social processes in larger and more legible scale. Take as a single instance the latter city. Its quick recovery has been called one of the wonders of the age. In the very midst of surrounding desolation and business extinction, the Californian city projected a Panama-Pacific exposition, and its citizens proceeded to arrange for one of the greatest of all world fairs. On the other hand, the social changes which succeed relatively small disturbances are often such as to elude an

[12] Ross, *op. cit.*, p. 200.

[13] To this cause of immobility may be added others, such as: (1) Narrow experience and few interests. (2) Large percentage of population owning property. (3) Oriental pride in permanence. (4) Fatalistic philosophies. (5) Over-emphasis of government.

[14] Thomas, *op. cit.*, pp. 20, 21.

estimate. The reason has been well suggested that "big crises bring changes about most easily because they affect all individuals alike at the same time." In other words a more general fluidity is accomplished. We see, therefore, a second principle begin to emerge. Not only is fluidity fundamental to social change, but the degree of fluidity seems to vary directly as the shock and extent of the catastrophe.

There yet remains to notice the bearing of catastrophe upon social progress. The following words are quotable in this connection:

> It is quite certain that the degree of progress of a people has a certain relation to the number of disturbances encountered, and the most progressive have had a more vicissitudinous life. Our proverb "Necessity is the mother of invention" is the formulation in folk-thought of this principle of social change.[15]

We cannot, however, remain long content with this suggestion as to the principle concerned—namely, that progress is a natural and an assured result of change. The point is that catastrophe always means social change. There is not always progress. It is well to guard against confusion here. Change means any qualitative variation, whereas progress means "amelioration, perfectionment." The latter will be seen to depend on other things—the nature of the shock, the models presented, the community culture and morale, the stimulus of leaders and lookers-on. The single case of Galveston, Texas,[16] is sufficient to disprove the too optimistic hypothesis that the effects of catastrophies are uniform. Here a city lost heart by reason of the overwhelming flood, and in spite of superior commercial advantages was outgrown by a rival fifty miles away. At the same time the case of Dayton, Ohio, should be borne in mind. Here also was a flood-stricken city and she became "the Gem City of the West." The principle[17] thus appears to be that progress in catastrophe is a resultant of specific conditioning factors, some of which are subject to social control.

It is indeed this very thing which makes possible the hope of eventual social control over disaster-stricken cities, and the transmutation of seeming evil into tremendous good. And this is in addition to the many practical social lessons which we have already been intelligent enough to preserve, such as those of better city-planning, and a more efficient charity organization.

How much of man's advancement has been directly or indirectly due to disaster?[18] The question asks itself and it is a question as yet without an answer. When

[15] Thomas, *op. cit.*, p. 18.

[16] "It has one of the finest, if not the finest, ports in North America. In 1900 a great tidal wave swept over the city, causing enormous damage and loss of life. While the city has had a certain growth since that time, it has been far outstripped by Houston, Dallas, and other Texas cities."—Kirby Page, formerly of Texas, in a letter to the author.

[17] Another principle is suggested for study by the following sentence in Ross' *Foundations of Sociology* (p. 206): "Brusk revolution in the conditions of life or thought produces not sudden, but gradual changes in society." This might easily be elaborated.

[18] The relationship of poetry and disaster is of interest. In a recent article on Disaster and Poetry a writer asks "whether often, if not always, suffering, disease and disaster do not bring to him [the poet] the will to create."—Marks, Jeanette, "Disaster and Poetry," *North American Review*, vol. 212, no. 1 (July, 1920), p. 93.

the answer is at last written, will there not be many surprises? Pitt-Rivers tells us that "the idea of a large boat might have been suggested in the time of floods when houses floated down the rivers before the eyes of men."[19] A terrible storm at sea gave America its first rice.[20] City-planning may be said to have taken its rise in America as a result of the Chicago fire, and the rôle of catastrophe in the progress of social legislation is a study in itself. The impetus thus received is immeasurable. Historically, labor-legislation took its rise with the coming of an infectious fever in the cotton-mills of Manchester in 1784. After the Cherry mine disaster legislation ensued at once. Again it was the Triangle fire which led to the appropriation of funds for a factory investigation commission in the State of New York. The sinking of the Titanic has greatly reduced the hazards of the sea.

It may easily prove true that the prophets of golden days to come who invariably arise on the day of disaster, are not entirely without ground for the faith which is in them; and that catastrophies are frequently only re-agents of further progress. But this is merely introductory. Thought becomes scientific only when its conclusions are checked up and under-written by observation or experiment. Prior to such procedure it must still remain opinion or belief.

The whole subject is, it must be repeated, a virgin field in sociology. Knowledge will grow scientific only after the most faithful examination of many catastrophies. But it must be realized that the data of the greatest value is left ofttimes unrecorded, and fades rapidly from the social memory. Investigation is needed immediately after the event. It is, therefore, of the utmost importance that sociological studies of Chicago, Galveston, Baltimore, San Francisco, and other disaster cities should be initiated at once.[21]

Of such a series—if the work can be done—this little volume on Halifax is offered as a beginning. It is hoped that the many inadequacies of treatment will receive the generous allowances permitted a pioneer.

[19] Thomas, *op. cit.*, p. 23.

[20] In this storm a ship from Madagascar was driven into a South Carolina port. In gratitude the Captain gave the Governor a sack of seed.

[21] It is perhaps due to the reader to say that while this volume treats specifically of Halifax, the writer has studied the records of many disasters and these have been kept in mind in drawing his conclusions. He participated in the rescue and relief work at Halifax in 1917, and at the time of the Titanic disaster accompanied one of the expeditions to the scene. He was in New York when the Wall Street explosion occurred, and made a first hand study of its effects.

CHAPTER I

CATASTROPHE AND SOCIAL DISINTEGRATION

The City of Halifax—Terrific nature of the explosion—Destruction of life and property—The subsequent fire and storms—Annihilation of homes—Arresting of business—Disintegration of the social order.

HALIFAX is the ocean terminal of the Dominion of Canada on her Atlantic seaboard. It is situated at the head of Chebucto Bay, a deep inlet on the southeastern shoreline of Nova Scotia. It is endowed by nature with a magnificent harbor, which as a matter of fact is one of the three finest in the world. In it a thousand vessels might safely ride at anchor. The possession of this harbor, together with ample defences, and a fortunate situation with regard to northern Europe established the Garrison City, early in the year 1914 as the natural war-base of the Dominion. Its tonnage leaped by millions, and it soon became the third shipping port in the entire British Empire. Hither the transports came, and the giant freighters to join their convoy. Cruisers and men-of-war put in to use its great dry-dock, or take on coal. Here too, cleared the supply and munition boats—some laden with empty shells, others with high explosives destined for the distant fields of battle. How much of the deadly cargo lay in the road-stead or came and went during those fateful years is not publicly known.[22] Certainly there was too much to breed a sense of safety, but no one gave the matter second thought. All were intent upon the mighty task of the hour. Sufficient unto each day was each day's evil. Each night the great war-gates were swung across the channels. Powerful searchlights swept unceasingly the sea and sky. The forts were fully manned. The gunners ready. The people knew these things, and no one dreamed of danger save to loved ones far away. Secure in her own defences the city lay unafraid, and almost apathetic.

About midway in the last two years of war—to be exact December, 1917,—a French munitioner[23] heavily laden with trinitrotoluol, the most powerful of known explosives, reached Halifax from New York. On the early morning of the sixth of that month, she was proceeding under her own steam up the harbor-length to-

[22] During the month of December, 1915, alone, 30,000 tons of munitions passed over the railroad piers of Halifax.

[23] The *Mont Blanc*, St. Nazaire, Captain Lemedec, Pilot Francis Mackay, owners La Compagnie General Transatlantique 3,121 tons gross, 2252 net register, steel, single screw, 330 ft. long, 40 ft. beam, speed 7½ to 8 knots, inward bound, from New York to await convoy. Cargo 450,000 lbs. trinitrotoluol, 2300 tons picric acid, 35 tons benzol, employed in carrying munitions to France.

ward anchorage in the basin—an oval expansion half-hidden by a blunt hill called Turple Head. Suddenly an empty Belgian relief ship[24] swept through the Narrows directly in her pathway. There was a confusion of signals; a few agonized manoeuvers. The vessels collided; and the shock of their colliding shook the world!

War came to America that morning. Two thousand slain, six thousand injured, ten thousand homeless, thirty-five millions of dollars in property destroyed, three hundred acres left a smoking waste, churches, schools, factories blown down or burned—such was the appalling havoc of the greatest single explosion in the history of the world.[25] It was an episode which baffles description. It is difficult to gain from words even an approximate idea of the catastrophe and what followed in its trail.

It was all of a sudden—a single devastating blast; then the sound as of the crashing of a thousand chandeliers. Men and women cowered under the shower of debris and glass. There was one awful moment when hearts sank, and breaths were held. Then women cried aloud, and men looked dumbly into each other's eyes, and awaited the crack of doom. To some death was quick and merciful in its coming. Others were blinded, and staggered to and fro before they dropped. Still others with shattered limbs dragged themselves forth into the light—naked, blackened, unrecognizable human shapes. They lay prone upon the streetside, under the shadow of the great death-cloud which still dropped soot and oil and water. It was truly a sight to make the angels weep.

Men who had been at the front said they had seen nothing so bad in Flanders. Over there men were torn with shrapnel, but the victims were in all cases men. Here father and mother, daughter and little child, all fell in "one red burial blent." A returned soldier said of it: "I have been in the trenches in France. I have gone over the top. Friends and comrades have been shot in my presence. I have seen scores of dead men lying upon the battlefield, but the sight .... was a thousand times worse and far more pathetic."[26] A well-known relief worker who had been at San Francisco, Chelsea and Salem immediately after those disasters said "I am impressed by the fact that this is much the saddest disaster I have seen." It has been compared to the scenes pictured by Lord Lytton in his tale of the last days of Pompeii:

> True there was not that hellish river of molten lava flowing down upon the fleeing people; and consuming them as feathers in fierce flames. But every other sickening detail was present—that of crashing shock and shaking earth, of crumbling homes, and cruel flame and fire. And there were showers, not it is true of ashes from the vortex of the volcano, but of soot and oil and water, of

[24] The *Imo*, Christiania, Captain Fron, Pilot William Hayes, owners Southern Pacific Whaling Company, 5,041 tons gross, 3161 tons register, steel, single screw, 430 ft. long, 45 ft. beam, speed 11 to 12 knots, outward bound to New York, in ballast, employed in carrying food to Belgium.

[25] The greatest previous explosion was when 500,000 pounds of dynamite blew up in Baltimore Harbor.

[26] Johnstone, Dwight, *The Tragedy of Halifax* (in MS.).

> death-dealing fragments of shrapnel and deck and boiler, of glass and wood and of the shattered ship.[27]

Like the New Albany tornado, it caused loss "in all five of the ways it is possible for a disaster to do so, in death, permanent injury, temporary injury, personal property loss, and real property loss."[28] Here were to be found in one dread assembling the combined horrors of war, earthquake, fire, flood, famine and storm—a combination seen for the first time in the records of human disaster.

It was an earthquake[29] so violent that when the explosion occurred the old, rock-founded city shook as with palsy. The citadel trembled, the whole horizon seemed to move with the passing of the earth waves. These were caught and registered, their tracings[30] carefully preserved, but the mute record tells not of the falling roofs and flying plaster and collapsing walls which to many an unfortunate victim brought death and burial at one and the same time.

It was a flood, for the sea rushed forward in a gigantic tidal wave, fully a fathom in depth. It swept past pier and embankment into the lower streets, and receding, left boats and wreckage high and dry, but carried to a watery doom score upon score of human lives. Nearly two hundred men were drowned.

It was a fire or rather a riot of fires, for the air was for a second filled with tongues of igneous vapour hiding themselves secretly within the lightning discharge of gas, only to burst out in gusts of sudden flame. Numberless buildings were presently ablaze. Soon there was naught to the northward but a roaring furnace. Above, the sky was crimson; below, a living crematorium—church and school, factory and home burned together in one fierce conflagration; and the brave firemen knew that there were men and women pinned beneath the wreckage, wounded past self-help. Frantic mothers heard the cries of little children, but in vain. Fathers desperately tore through burning brands, but often failed to save alive the captives of the flame. And so the last dread process went on,—earth to earth, ashes to ashes, dust to dust. And when the fires at last abated, the north end of the City of Halifax looked like some blackened hillside which a farmer had burned for fallow in the spring.

But perhaps the most terrible of all the terrible accompaniments was the tornado-like gas-blast from the bursting ship. It wrought instant havoc everywhere. Trees were torn from the ground. Poles were snapped like toothpicks. Trains were stopped dead. Cars were left in twisted masses. Pedestrians were thrown violently into the air, houses collapsed on all sides. Steamers were slammed against the docks. Then followed a veritable air-raid, when the sky rained iron fragments upon the helpless city. Like a meteoric shower of death, they fell piercing a thousand roofs, and with many a mighty splash bore down into the sea.

---

[27] McGlashen, Rev. J. A., *The Patriot* (Dartmouth, N. S.).

[28] Deacon, J. Byron, *Disasters* (N. Y., 1918), ch. ii, p. 158.

[29] "The effect of the vast, sudden interference with the air was practically the same as if an earthquake had shaken Halifax to the ground." (MacMechan, Archibald, "Halifax in Ruins," *The Canadian Courier*, vol. xxiii, no. 4, p. 6.)

[30] The tracings on the seismograph show three distinct shocks at the hours 9.05, 9.10 and 10.05.

Nor yet did this complete the tale of woes of this *Dies Irae*. Scarce was the catastrophe an hour old when the news was flashed around that a second explosion was approaching. It was the powder magazine in the Navy-yard, and the flames were perilously near. Through the crowded streets raced the heralds like prophets of wrath to come. "Flee!.... Flee!.... Get into the open ground" was the cry. Shops were abandoned unguarded, goods laid open on every side. No key was turned, no till was closed, but all instanter joined the precipitant throng, driven like animals before a prairie fire—yet this was not all; for "the plight of the aged, the sick, the infants, the bed-ridden, the cripples, the nursing mothers, the pregnant can not be described."

It was like the flight from Vesuvius of which Pliny the Younger tells:

> You could hear the shrieks of women, the crying of children and the shouts of men. Some were seeking their children; others their parents, others their wives and husbands ... one lamenting his own fate, another that of his family. Some praying to die from the very fear of dying, many lifting their hands to the gods, but the greater part imagining that there were no gods left anywhere, and that the last and eternal night was come upon the world.[31]

It has been said that "Moscow was no more deserted before Napoleon than were the shattered streets of Halifax when this flight had been carried out."[32] And when the hegira was over, and when there had ensued a partial recovery from the blow and gloom, a still lower depth of agony had yet to be undergone—a succession of winter storms. Blizzards, rain, floods and zero weather were even then upon the way. They came in close procession and as if to crown and complete the terrors of the great catastrophe thunder rumbled, lightning broke sharply and lit up weirdly the snow-clad streets. Such was the catastrophe of Halifax—"a calamity the appalling nature of which stirred the imagination of the world."[33]

The description here concluded, brief and inadequate as it is, will sufficiently indicate the terrific nature of the catastrophic shock, and explain how utter and complete was the social disintegration which followed.

There was the disintegration of the home and the family,—the reproductive system of society—its members sundered and helpless to avert it. There was the disintegration of the regulative system—government was in perplexity, and streets were without patrol. There was the disintegration of the sustaining system—a dislocation of transportation, a disorganization of business while the wheels of industry ceased in their turning. There was a derangement of the distributive system[34]—of all the usual services, of illumination, water-connections, telephones, deliveries. It was impossible to communicate with the outside world. There were no cars, no mails, no wires. There was a time when the city ceased to be a city, its citizens a mass of unorganized units—struggling for safety, shelter, covering and bread. As Lytton wrote of Pompeii; "The whole elements of civilization were bro-

[31] Pliny, *Letters* (London, 1915), vol. i, bk. vi, p. 495.

[32] Smith, Stanley K., *The Halifax Horror* (Halifax, 1918), ch. ii, p. 24.

[33] Bell, McKelvie, *A Romance of the Halifax Disaster* (Halifax, 1918), p. 57.

[34] Spencer, Herbert, *The Principles of Sociology* (N. Y., 1908), pt. ii, p. 499 *et seq.*

ken up .... nothing in all the varied and complicated machinery of social life was left save the primal law of self preservation."[35]

A writer has given a vivid word picture of the social contrasts of the disaster night and the beautiful evening before.

> What a change from the night before! No theatres open, no happy throngs along the street, no cheery gatherings around the fire-side. The houses were all cold, and dark and silent. Instead of laughter, weeping; instead of dancing, agonizing pain; instead of Elysian dreams, ominous nightmares. Fears and sorrow were in the way and all the daughters of music were brought low ... Halifax had become in a trice a city of dead bodies, ruined homes and blasted hopes.[36]

To have looked in upon one of the great makeshift dormitories that first night, to have seen men, women and children, of all stations, huddled together on the stages of theatres, the chancels of churches, in stables, box-cars and basements was to have beheld a rift in the social structure such as no community had ever known. Old traditional social lines were hopelessly mixed and confused. The catastrophe smashed through strong walls like cobwebs, but it also smashed through fixed traditions, social divisions and old standards, making a rent which would not easily repair. Rich and poor, debutante and chambermaid, official and bellboy met for the first time as victims of a common calamity.

Even on the eighth, two days after the disaster, when Mr. Ratshesky of the Massachusetts' Relief arrived he could report: "An awful sight presented itself, buildings shattered on all sides—chaos apparent." In a room in the City Hall twelve by twenty, he found assembled "men and women trying to organize different departments of relief, while other rooms were filled to utmost capacity with people pleading for doctors, nurses, food, and clothing for themselves and members of their families. Everything was in turmoil."[37] This account faithfully expresses the disintegration which came with the great shock of what had come to pass. It is this disintegration and the resultant phenomena which are of utmost importance for the student of social science to observe. To be quite emotionally free in the observation of such phenomena, however, is almost impossible. It has been said of sociological investigations that

> observation is made under bias because the facts under review are those of human life and touch human interest. A man can count the legs of a fly without having his heart wrung because he thinks there are too many or too few. But when he observes the life of the society in which he moves, lives and has his being, or some other society nearby, it is the rule that he approves or disapproves, is edified or horrified, by what he observes. When he does that he

[35] Lytton, Lord, *The Last Days of Pompeii* (London, 1896), p. 405.

[36] Johnstone, *op. cit.*

[37] Ratshesky, A. C., "Report of Halifax Relief Expedition," *The State* (Boston, 1918), p. 11.

passes a moral judgment.[38]

Sociology has suffered because of this inevitable bias. In our present study it is natural that our sympathy reactions should be especially strong. "*Quamquam animus meminisse horret, incipiam*" must be our motto. As students we must now endeavor to dissociate ourselves from them, and look upon the stricken Canadian city with all a chemist's patient detachment. In a field of science where the prospect of large-scale experimental progress is remote, we must learn well when the abnormal reveals itself in great tragedies and when social processes are seen magnified by a thousand diameters. Only thus can we hope for advances that will endure.

In this spirit then let us watch the slow process of the reorganization of Halifax, and see in it a picture of society itself as it reacts under the stimulus of catastrophe, and adjusts itself to the circumstantial pressure of new conditions.

Before doing so, however, we shall pause, in the next chapter, to glance at a number of social phenomena which should be recorded and examined in the light of social psychology. But we must not lose the relationship of each chapter to our major thesis. It is sufficient for our purpose if thus far it has been shown that at Halifax the shock resulted in disintegration of social institutions, dislocation of the usual methods of social control and dissolution of the customary; that through the catastrophe the community was thrown into the state of flux which, as was suggested in the introduction, is the logical and natural prerequisite for social change; and finally that the shock was of a character such as "to affect all individuals alike at the same time," and to induce that degree of fluidity most favorable to social change.

---

[38] Keller, A. G., "Sociology and Science," *The Nation* (N. Y., May 4, 1916), vol. 102, no. 2653, p. 275.

CHAPTER II

CATASTROPHE AND SOCIAL PSYCHOLOGY

Shock reaction—Hallucination—Primitive instincts—Crowd psychology—Phenomena of emotion—How men react when bereft completely—Post-catastrophic phenomena—Human nature in the absence of repression by conventionality, custom and law—Fatigue and the human will—The stimuli of heroism—Mutual aid.

Social Psychology is a subject of primary importance to the student of society. Like Sociology itself its field is far from being exhausted. One looks in vain for a treatment of disaster psychology. In such a study the diverse phenomena involved would be of interest to the psychologist. Their effects in retarding or promoting social organization would concern the sociologist. With such possible effects in mind we are now to proceed to an examination of the major subjective reactions as they were to be seen in the Halifax catastrophe.

It is improbable that any single community has ever presented so composite a picture of human traits in such bold relief as appeared in the City of Halifax upon the day of the explosion. Human phenomena which many knew of only as hidden away in books, stood out so clearly that he who ran might read. Besides the physiological reactions there was abundant illustration of hallucination, delusion, primitive instincts, and crowd psychology as well of other phenomena all of which have important sociological significance tending either to prolong disintegration, or to hasten social recovery.

The first of these phenomena was the "stun" of the catastrophe itself. The shock reaction at Halifax has been variously described. It has been graphically likened "to being suddenly stricken with blindness and paralysis." It was a sensation of utter helplessness and disability. "We died a thousand horrible deaths" ran one description, "the nervous shock and terror were as hard to bear as were the wounds." "The people are dazed," wrote another observer, "they have almost ceased to exercise the sensation of pain." This physiological reaction animals and men shared alike. The appearance of the terror-stricken horses was as of beasts which had suddenly gone mad.

A physiological accompaniment of shock and distraction is the abnormal action of the glands. The disturbance of the sympathetic nervous system produced by the emotional stress and strain of a great excitement or a great disappointment is reflected in the stimulation or inhibition of glandular action. Much physical as well as nervous illness was precipitated by the grief, excitement and exposure of the disaster.[39] Among cases observed were those of diabetes, tuberculosis and hyper-thyroidism, as well as the nervous instability to which reference is subsequently made. Such an epidemic of hyper-thyroidism—exaggerated action of the thyroid gland—is said to have followed the Kishineff massacres, the San Francisco earthquake and the air-raids on London.[40] As to diabetes, it has been shown that

> emotions cause increased output of glycogen. Glycogen is a step toward diabetes and therefore this disease is prone to appear in persons under emotional strain ... so common is this particular result in persons under prolonged emotion that someone has said that "when stocks go down in New York, diabetes goes up."[41]

Turning now to other psychological aspects, we have to note the presence of hallucination in disaster.

> Hallucination may be roughly defined as false sense impression. For example, the patient sees an object which has no real existence, or hears an imaginary voice. Hallucinations are termed visual, auditory, tactile, *etc.* according to the sense to which the false impression appears to belong.[42]

Hallucination is induced by the unusual suggesting the expected. It is sense-perception colored by association. It is the power of a dominant idea that, unbidden, enters the field of consciousness and takes possession of even the senses themselves. In Halifax one idea seemed to dominate most minds and clothe itself in the semblance of reality—the expected Germans. For a long time there had been under public discussion the question as to whether or not the city would be shelled by Zeppelin raiders, or possibly by a fleet at sea. All street-lights had been darkened by military orders. The failure to draw window shades had been subject to heavy penalty. It is no wonder eyes looked upward when there came the crash, and when seeing the strange unusual cloud beheld the Zeppelin of fancy. A man residing on the outskirts of the town of Dartmouth "heard" a German shell pass shrieking above him. Dartmouth Heights looks out over Halifax harbor, and here perhaps the vista is most expansive, and the eye sees furthest. The instant after the explosion a citizen standing here "saw" clearly a German fleet manoeuvering in the distance.[43] That shells had actually come few on the instant doubted. The head of one firm advised his employees not to run elsewhere, as "two shots never fall in the same place."

---

[39] For a full discussion of nervous disorders induced by an explosion at short range, *vide* Roussy and Llermette, *The Psychoneuroses of War* (London, 1918), ch. x.

[40] Brown, W. Langden, Presidential address to Hunterian Society, London.

[41] Crile, George W., *The Origin and Nature of the Emotions* (Phila., 1915), p. 163.

[42] Hart, Bernard, *The Psychology of Insanity* (Cambridge, 1916), ch. iii, p. 30.

[43] "So hypochondriac fancies represent
Ships, armies, battles in the firmament
Till steady eyes the exhalations solve
And all to its first matter, cloud, resolve."

—Defoe, *Journal of the Plague Year*.

This—a German assault—was the great mental explanation that came into the majority of minds. There was one other—that of the end of the world. Many fell to their knees in prayer. One woman was found in the open yard by her broken home repeating the general confession of the church. Few would have been surprised if out of the smoky cloud-ridden skies there should have appeared the archangels announcing the consummation of mundane affairs. Indeed there were instances, not a few, of those who "saw" in the death-cloud "the clear outlines of a face." Thus both auditory and visual hallucination were manifested to a degree.

Hallucination has been described as "seeing" something which has no basis in reality. Thus it differs from delusion, which is rather a misinterpretation of what is seen. "Delusions are closely allied to hallucinations and generally accompany the latter. The distinction lies in the fact that delusions are not false sensations but false beliefs."[44] Anxiety, distraction by grief and loss, as well as nervous shock play freely with the mind and fancy and often swerve the judgment of perception. This was especially noticeable at Halifax in the hospital identification, particularly of children. A distracted father looked into a little girl's face four different times but did not recognize her as his own which, in fact, she was. The precisely opposite occurrence was also noted. A fond parent time and time again "discovered" his lost child, "seeing" to complete satisfaction special marks and features on its little body. But often there were present those who knew better, and the better judgment prevailed. Again this phenomenon was repeated in numberless instances at the morgue. Wearied and white after frantic and fruitless search wherever refugees were gathered together, the overwrought searchers would walk through the long lines of dead, and suddenly "recognize" a missing relative or friend.[45] Regretfully the attendant fulfilled the same thankless task from day to day. There had been no recognition at all. The observer had seen "not the object itself but the image evoked in the mind."[46]

The primitive instincts of man were for a long time vaguely and loosely defined, until James and later McDougall essayed to give them name and number. But only with Thorndike's critical examination has it become clear how difficult a thing it is to carry the analysis of any situation back to the elemental or "primal movers of all human activity." Thorndike is satisfied to describe them as nothing save a set of original tendencies to respond to stimuli in more or less definite directions. When he speaks of instincts it is to mean only a "series of situations and responses" or "a set of tendencies for various situations to arouse the feelings of fear, anger, pity, *etc.* with which certain bodily movements usually go." Among them, there are those resulting in "food-getting and habitation," in "fear, fighting and anger" and in "human intercourse."[47] But McDougall's classification preserves the old phrases, and men are likely to go on speaking of the "instinct of flight," the "instinct of pugnacity," "parental instinct," "gregarious instinct" and

[44] Hart, *op. cit.*, ch. iii, p. 31.

[45] For parallel cases of erroneous recognition of the dead, *vide* Le Bon, Gustave, *The Crowd, a Study of the Popular Mind* (London), bk. i, ch. i, p. 51.

[46] *Ibid.*, p. 51.

[47] Thorndike, Edward L., *The Original Nature of Man* (N. Y., 1913), ch. v, p. 43 *et seq.*

the others.[48] For the sociologist it is enough that all agree that men are held under some powerful grip of nature and driven at times almost inevitably to the doing of acts quite irrespective of their social effects.

In catastrophe these primitive instincts are seen most plainly and less subject to the re-conditioning influences of ordinary life. This was especially noticeable at Halifax. The instinct of flight for self-preservation was reflected in the reaction of thousands. "Almost without thought, probably from the natural instinct of self-preservation I backed from the window to a small store-room and stood there dazed."[49] The experience so described may be said to have been general. This instinct was to be seen again in the action of the crew of the explosives-laden ship. Scarcely had the collision occurred when the whole complement lowered away the boats, rowed like madmen to the nearest shore—which happened to be that opposite to Halifax—and "scooted for the woods." As the ship, although set on fire immediately after the impact, did not actually blow up until some twenty minutes later, much might have been done by men less under the domination of instinct, in the way of warning and perhaps of minimizing the inevitable catastrophe.[50]

The instinct of pugnacity was to be seen in many a fine example of difficulty overcome in the work of rescue; as also in other instances, some suggestive of that early combat when animals and men struggled for mere physical existence.

The parental instinct was everywhere in evidence, and was reflected not only in the sacrifices made and the privations endured by parents for their young, but in every act of relief, which arose in involuntary response to the cry of the distressed. It perhaps partially explains the phenomenon often noticed in disasters that "immediately and spontaneously neighbors and fellow-townsmen spring to the work of rescue and first aid."[51]

The gregarious instinct—the instinct to herd—showed itself in the spontaneous groupings which came about and which seemed somehow to be associated with feelings of security from further harm. The refugees found comfort in the group. They rarely remained alone.

These and other instinctive responses in a greater or less degree of complication were to be remarked of the actions not only of individuals but of groups as well. In the latter the typical phenomena of crowd psychology were manifested upon every hand. The crowd was seen to be what it is—"the like response of many to a socially inciting event or suggestion such as sudden danger." Out of a mere agglomeration of individuals and under the stress of emotional excitement there arose that mental unity, which Le Bon emphasizes.[52] There was noticeable

[48] McDougall, William, *An Introduction to Social Psychology* (Boston, 1917), ch. iii, p. 49 *et seq.*

[49] Sheldon, J., *The Busy East* (Sackville, N. B. Can.), March, 1918.

[50] The judgment of the court of enquiry ran as follows: "The master and pilot of the Mont Blanc are guilty of neglect of public safety in not taking proper steps to warn the inhabitants of the city of a probable explosion." (Drysdale Commission, *Judgment of,* sec. viii.)

[51] Deacon, J. Byron, *Disasters* (N. Y., 1918), ch. vi, p. 151.

[52] Le Bon, *op. cit.*, p. 26.

the feeling of safety associated with togetherness which Trotter suggests.[53] There was the suggestibility, with its preceding conditions which Sidis[54] has clarified, namely, expectancy, inhibition, and limitation of the field of consciousness. There were the triple characteristics which Giddings notes: "Crowds are subject to swift contagion of feeling, they are sensitive to suggestion .... and always manifest a tendency to carry suggested ideas immediately into action."[55]

Of illustrations of impulsive social action there are none more apt than those furnished by the reactions following the Halifax tragedy. Only Pliny's narrative of the flight from the eruption of Vesuvius, or the story of the "Day of Fear" in France,[56] or that depicting the days of the comet[57] are comparable thereto.

At first all was confusion. Some ran to the cellars. Some ran to the streets. Some ran to their shops. Those in the shops ran home. This was in the area of wounds and bruises. Farther north was the area of death. Thither the rescuers turned. Automobiles sped over broken glass and splintered boards toward the unknown. Then came the orders of the soldiers, whose barracks were situated in the very heart of the danger district, for the people to fly southward, Common-ward, to the open spaces—anywhere. Another explosion was imminent. Then came further outbreaks of the flight impulse. Runs a graphic account:

> The crowd needed no second warning. They turned and fled. Hammers, shovels and bandages were thrown aside. Stores were left wide open with piles of currency on their counters. Homes were vacated in a twinkling. Little tots couldn't understand why they were being dragged along so fast. Some folks never looked back. Others did, either to catch a last glimpse of the home they never expected to see again or to tell if they could from the sky how far behind them the Dreaded Thing was.... They fled as they were.... Some carried children or bundles of such things as they had scrambled together.... Many were but scantily clad. Women fled in their night dresses. A few were stark naked, their bodies blackened with soot and grime. These had come from the destroyed section of the North End. What a storm-tossed motley throng, and as varied in its aspect and as poignant in its sufferings as any band of Belgian or Serbian refugees fleeing before the Hun.... A few rode in autos, but the great majority were on foot. With blanched faces, bleeding bodies and broken hearts, they fled from the Spectral Death they thought was coming hard after, fled to the open spaces where possibly its shadow might not fall. Soon Citadel Hill and the Common were black with terrified thousands. Thousands more trudged along St. Margaret's Bay road, seeking escape among its trees and winding curves.... Many cut down boughs and made themselves fires—for they were bitterly

[53] Trotter, William, *Instincts of the Herd in Peace and War* (London, 1919), p. 31.
[54] Sidis, Boris, *The Psychology of Suggestion* (N. Y., 1919), ch. vi, p. 56 *et seq.*
[55] Giddings, Franklin H., *Principles of Sociology* (N. Y., 1916), bk. ii, ch. ii, p. 136.
[56] Stephens, Henry M., *A History of the French Revolution* (N. Y., 1886), vol. i, p. 179.
[57] Wells, H. G., *In the Days of the Comet* (N. Y., 1906).

> cold. Here they were—poorly clad, badly wounded, and with not one loaf of bread in all their number, so hastily did they leave, when galloping horsemen announced the danger was over and it was safe to return.[58]

The ever-shifting responsiveness to rumor which distinguishes a crowd was noted.

> The entrance to the Park was black with human beings, some massed in groups, some running anxiously back and forth like ants when their hill has been crushed. There were blanched faces and trembling hands. The wildest rumors were in circulation and every bearer of tidings was immediately surrounded.[59]

Not only here but when the crowd trekked back, and in the subsequent scenes which were witnessed in supply stations and shelters, the association which Sidis draws between calamity and hyper-suggestibility in the body politic was abundantly endorsed.

We must now endeavor to understand the phenomena of emotion which accompany a great catastrophe. This is not the less difficult because the term emotion is not given consistent use even by psychologists. One interprets it as merely the affective side of the instinctive process—those "modes of affective experience," such as "anger, fear, curiosity," which accompany the excitement of "the principal powerful instincts."[60] Another sees it as also an impulsive, not merely a receptive state. It is "the way the body feels when it is prepared for a certain reaction," and includes "an impulse toward the particular reaction."[61]

It will be accurate enough for our purpose to think of the emotions as complicated states of feeling more or less allied to one another and to the human will.[62] Among them are jealousy and envy—"discomfort at seeing others approved and at being out-done by them."[63] This appeared repeatedly in the administration of relief and should be included in disaster psychology. Again greed[64]—more strictly a social instinct than an emotion—was common. How common will receive further exemplification in a later chapter.

Fear has already been referred to. Anger, shame, resentment while evident, were of less significance. Gratitude was early shown and there were many formal expressions of it. Later on, it seemed to be replaced by a feeling that as sufferers

[58] Johnstone, Dwight, *The Tragedy of Halifax* (in MS.).

[59] *St. John Globe*, Correspondence, Dec., 1917.

[60] McDougall, *op. cit.*, p. 46.

[61] Woodworth, Robert S., *Dynamic Psychology* (N. Y., 1918), ch. iii, p. 54.

[62] "Anger, zeal, determination, willing, are closely allied, and probably identical in part. Certainly they are aroused by the same stimulus, namely, by obstruction, encountered in the pursuit of some end." (*Ibid.*, p. 149.)

[63] Thorndike, *op. cit.*, p. 101.

[64] "To go for attractive objects, to grab them when within reach, to hold them against competitors, to fight the one who tries to take them away. To go for, grab and hold them all the more if another is trying to do so, these lines of conduct are the roots of greed." (*Ibid.*, p. 102.)

they, the victims, were only receiving their due in whatever aid was obtained.

Of special interest is the rôle of the tender emotions, kindliness, sympathy and sorrow, as well as the reactions which may be expected when these occur in unusual exaltation through the repetition of stimuli or otherwise. Whatever may be the nature of the process whereby the feelings of his fellows affect a man, that which chiefly concerns us here, is how these reactions differ when the stimulation is multiplex. Of this multiplex stimulation in collective psychology Graham Wallas has written:

> The nervous exaltation so produced may be the effect of the rapid repetition of stimuli acting as repetition acts, for instance, when it produces seasickness or tickling.... If the exaltation is extreme conscious control of feeling and action is diminished.[65] Reaction is narrowed and men may behave, as they behave in dreams, less rationally and morally than they do if the whole of their nature is brought into play.[66]

What Wallas has said of the additional stimulation which the presence of a crowd induces may be given wider application, and is indeed a most illuminating thought, describing exactly the psycho-emotional reactions produced by the stimulation of terrifying scenes, such as were witnessed at Halifax.

A case in point was that of the nervous exaltation produced upon a young doctor who operated continuously for many hours in the removal of injured eyes. The emotional tension he went through is expressed in his words to a witness: "If relief doesn't come to me soon, I shall murder somebody."

Another instance where conscious control of feeling and action was diminished was that of a soldier. He was so affected by what he passed through during the explosion and his two days' participation in relief work, that he quite unwittingly took a seat in a train departing for Montreal. Later in a hospital of that city after many mental wanderings he recovered his memory. Over and over again he had been picturing the dreadful scenes which he had experienced. This condition includes a hyperactivity of the imagination "characterized by oneirism [oneiric delirium] reproducing most often the tragic or terrible scenes which immediately preceded the hypogenic shock."[67]

The nature of sympathy[68] may not be clearly comprehended but of its effects there is no doubt. It may lead to the relief of pain or induce the exactly opposite effect; or it may bring about so lively a distress as to quite incapacitate a man from

[65] M. Dide, a French psychologist, regards "the hypnosis produced by emotional shock—and this occurs not only in war but in other great catastrophies as well—as genetically a defence reaction, like natural sleep whose function according to him is primarily prophylactic against exhaustion and fatigue, ... it is comparable to the so-called death-shamming of animals." (Dide, M., *Les émotions et la guerre* (Paris, 1918), Review of, *Psychological Bulletin,* vol. xv, no. 12, Dec., 1918, p. 441.)

[66] Wallas, Graham, *The Great Society* (N. Y., 1917), p. 136.

[67] *Ibid.,* p. 440.

[68] Classed by William James as an emotion, but considered by McDougall a pseudo-instinct.

giving help. Again it may lead to the avoidance of disaster scenes altogether. Thus some could on no account be prevailed upon to go into the hospitals or to enter the devastated area. Others by a process understood in the psychology of insanity secured the desired avoidance by suicide. The association of suicide with catastrophe has been already remarked in the case of San Francisco. A Halifax instance was that of a physician who had labored hard among the wounded. He later found the reaction of his emotional experiences too strong. He lost his mental balance and was discovered dead one morning near his office door. He had hanged himself during the night. Still another, a railroad man, driven to despair by loneliness and loss, his wife and children having perished, attempted to follow them in death.

Joy and sorrow are pleasure-pain conditions of emotional states. Sorrow is painful because "the impulse is baffled and cannot attain more than the most scanty and imperfect satisfaction in little acts, such as the leaving of flowers on the grave;"[69] although the intensity is increased by other considerations. Here again the unusual degree of stimulation which catastrophe induces brings about a behavior other than that which commonly attends the experience of grief. A phenomenon associated with wholesale bereavement is the almost entire absence of tears. A witness of the San Francisco disaster said it was at the end of the second day that he saw tears for the first time.[70] At Halifax, where the loss of life was many times greater, there was little crying. There seemed to be indeed a miserable but strong consolation in the fact that all were alike involved in the same calamity.[71]

There was "no bitterness, no complaint, only a great and eager desire to help some one less fortunate." Another observer said: "I have never seen such kindly feeling. I have never seen such tender sympathy. I have never heard an impatient word." And this was amongst men "who were covered with bruises, and whose hearts were heavy, who have not had a night's sleep, and who go all day long without thought of food." Another visitor remarked "there is not a more courageous, sane and reasonable people. Everyone is tender and considerate. Men who have lost wives and children, women whose sons and husbands are dead, boys and girls whose homes have been destroyed, are working to relieve the distress." A Montreal clergyman reported that "Halifax people have been meeting with dry eyes and calm faces the tragedies, the horrors, the sufferings and the exposures which followed the explosion." Grief is after all "a passive emotion," a "reaction of helplessness." It is "a state of mind appropriate to a condition of affairs where nothing is to be done"—[72] and there was much to be done at Halifax.

There are also to be added the phenomena of emotional parturition. As was to be expected the shock meant the immediate provision of a maternity hospital. Babies were born in cellars and among ruins. Premature births were common, one indeed taking place in the midst of the huddled thousands of refugees waiting in anguish upon the Common for permission to return to their abandoned homes.

[69] McDougall, *op. cit.*, p. 152.

[70] O'Connor, Chas. J., *San Francisco Relief Survey* (N. Y., 1913), pt. i, p. 6.

[71] "The cutting edge of all our usual misfortunes comes from their character of loneliness."—(James, William, *Memories and Studies*, N. Y., 1911, p. 224.)

[72] Woodworth, *op. cit.*, p. 58.

Nor were all the ills for which the shock was responsible immediately discernible. There were many post-catastrophic phenomena. Three months after the explosion many found themselves suffering an inexplicable breakdown, which the doctors attributed unquestionably to the catastrophe. It was a condition closely allied to "war-neurasthenia." Another disaster after-effect also may be here recorded. This was the not unnatural way in which people "lived on edge," for a long period after the disaster. There was a readiness and suggestibility to respond to rumor or to the least excitant. Twice at least the schools were emptied precipitately, and citizens went forth into pell-mell flight from their homes upon the circulation of reports of possible danger. No better illustration is afforded of the sociological fact that "the more expectant, or overwrought the public mind, the easier it is to set up a great perturbation. After a series of public calamities .... minds are blown about by every gust of passion or sentiment."[73]

There are also to be included a few miscellaneous observations of behavior associated with the psychology of disaster relief. (1) The preference upon the part of the refugee for plural leadership and decision. (2) The aggravation of helplessness through the open distribution of relief. (3) The resentment which succeeds the intrusion of strangers in relief leadership. (4) The reaction of lassitude and depression after a period of strain. (5) The desire for privacy during interviews. (6) The vital importance of prompt decision in preventing an epidemic of complaint.[74]

Analytic psychology is becoming increasingly interested in the phenomena of repression, inhibition and taboo. The real motives of action are often very different from the apparent motives which overlie them. Instinctive tendencies are buried beneath barriers of civilization, but they are buried alive. They are covered not crushed. These resistances are either within our minds or in society. The latter are summed up in conventionality, custom and law, all so relatively recent[75] in time as to supply a very thin veneer over the primitive tendencies which have held sway for ages. Few realize the place which conventionality, custom and law possess in a community until in some extraordinary catastrophe their power is broken, or what is the same thing the ability to enforce them is paralyzed. This fact is especially true of repressive enactments, and most laws fall within this category. Catastrophe shatters the unsubstantial veneer. When the police of Boston went on strike it was not only the signal for the crooks of all towns to repair to the unguarded center, but an unexpected reserve of crookedness came to light within the city itself. Lytton discovered at Pompeii signs of plunder and sacrilege which had taken place "when the pillars of the world tottered to and fro." At the time of the St. John Fire "loafers and thieves held high carnival. All night long they roamed the streets and thieved upon the misfortunes of others."[76]

With the possibility of apprehension reduced to a minimum in the confusion

[73] Ross, Edward A., *Social Psychology* (N. Y., 1918), ch. iv, p. 66.

[74] A list compiled by the author from suggestions in Deacon's discussion of disasters. All were to be observed at Halifax.

[75] It has been said that were the period of man's residence on earth considered as having covered an hundred thousand years, that of civilization would be represented by the last ten minutes.

[76] Stewart, George, *The Story of the Great Fire in St. John* (Toronto, 1877), p. 35.

at Halifax, with the deterrent forces of respectability and law practically unknown, men appeared for what they were as the following statement only too well discloses:

> Few folk thought that Halifax harbored any would-be ghouls or vultures. The disaster showed how many. Men clambered over the bodies of the dead to get beer in the shattered breweries. Men taking advantage of the flight from the city because of the possibility of another explosion went into houses and shops, and took whatever their thieving fingers could lay hold of. Then there were the nightly prowlers among the ruins, who rifled the pockets of the dead and dying, and snatched rings from icy fingers. A woman lying unconscious on the street had her fur coat snatched from her back.... One of the workers, hearing some one groaning rescued a shop-keeper from underneath the debris. Unearthing at the same time a cash box containing one hundred and fifty dollars, he gave it to a young man standing by to hold while he took the victim to a place of refuge. When he returned the box was there, but the young man and the money had disappeared.
>
> Then there was the profiteering phase. Landlords raised their rents upon people in no position to bear it. The Halifax Trades and Labor Council adopted a resolution urging that the Mayor be authorized to request all persons to report landlords who "have taken advantage of conditions created by the explosion." ... Plumbers refused to hold their union rules in abeyance and to work one minute beyond the regular eight hours unless they received their extra rates for overtime; and the bricklayers assumed a dog-in-the-manger attitude and refused to allow the plasterers to help in the repair of the chimneys. And this during days of dire stress ... when many men and women were working twelve and fourteen hours a day without a cent or thought of remuneration. One Halifax newspaper spoke of these men as "squeezing the uttermost farthing out of the anguished necessities of the homeless men, women and children." Truckmen charged exorbitant prices for the transferring of goods and baggage. Merchants boosted prices. A small shopkeeper asked a little starving child thirty cents for a loaf of bread.
>
> On Tuesday, December the twelfth, the Deputy Mayor issued a proclamation warning persons so acting that they would be dealt with under the provisions of the law.[77]

Slowly the arm of repression grew vigorous once more. The military placed troops on patrol. Sentries were posted preventing entrance to the ruins to those who were not supplied with a special pass. Orders were issued to shoot any looter trying to escape. The Mayor's proclamation, the warning of the relief committee, the storm of popular indignation gradually became effectual.

[77] Johnstone, *op. cit.*

The stimulus of the same catastrophe, it thus appears, may result in two different types of responses—that of greed on the one hand or altruistic emotion on the other. One individual is spurred to increased activity by the opportunity of business profit, another by the sense of social needs. Why this is so—indeed the whole field of profiteering—would be a subject of interesting enquiry. Whether it is due to the varying degrees of socialization represented in the different individuals or whether it is not also partly due to the fact that philanthropy functions best in a sphere out of line with a man's own particular occupation, the truth remains that some display an altogether unusual type of reaction in an emergency to the actions of others; and perhaps exhibit behavior quite different from that which appears normal in a realm of conduct where associations based on habit are so strongly ingrained.

The human will as we have seen is in close association with the emotions. We are now to notice the dynamogenic value of the strong emotions aroused by catastrophe. It is first of all essential to remember the rôle of adrenin in counteracting the effects of fatigue. Wonderful phenomena of endurance in disaster might well be anticipated for "adrenin set free in pain and in fear and in rage would put the members of the body unqualifiedly at the disposal of the nervous system." This is "living on one's will" or on "one's nerve." There are "reservoirs" of power ready to pour forth streams of energy if the occasion presents itself. Strong emotions may become an "arsenal of augmented strength." This fact William James was quick to see when he said "on any given day there are energies slumbering within us which the incitements of that day do not call forth."[78] But it was left to Cannon to unfold the physiological reasons,[79] and for Woodworth to explain how the presence of obstruction has power to call forth new energies.[80] Indeed the will[81] is just the inner driving force of the individual and an effort of will is only "the development of fresh motor power."[82] Following the lines of least resistance the will experiences no unusual exercise. Catastrophe opposes the tendency to eliminate from life everything that requires a calling forth of unusual energies.

The energizing influence of an emotional excitant was shown at Halifax in the remarkable way in which sick soldiers abandoned their beds and turned them over to the victims rushed to the military hospitals. It was seen again in the sudden accession of strength displayed by the invalids and the infirm during the hurried evacuation of the houses—a behavior like that of the inhabitants of Antwerp during the bombardment of that city in October 1914, when those who fled to Holland showed extraordinary resistance to fatigue.[83] The resistance to fatigue and suffering received more abundant illustration at Halifax in the work of rescue

[78] James, William, *The Energies of Men* (N. Y., 1920), p. 11.

[79] Cannon, Walter B., *Bodily changes in Pain, Hunger, Fear and Rage*, ch. xi, p. 184, *et seq.*

[80] Woodworth, *op. cit.*, p. 147.

[81] Will is indeed the supreme faculty, the whole mind in action, the internal stimulus which may call forth all the capacities and powers. (Conklin, Edwin G., *Heredity and Environment in the Development of Man* [Princeton], ch. vi, p. 47.)

[82] Woodworth, *op. cit.*, p. 149.

[83] Sano, F., "Documenti della guerra: Osservazioni psicologiche notate durante il bombardamento di Anversa," *Rivista di psichologia*, anno xi, pp. 119–128.

and relief. Often men themselves were surprised at their own power for prolonged effort and prodigious strain under the excitement of catastrophe. It was only on Monday (the fifth day) that collapses from work began to appear. Among the more generally known instances of unusual endurance was that of a private, who with one of his eyes knocked out, continued working the entire day of the disaster. Another was that of a chauffeur who with a broken rib conveyed the wounded trip after trip to the hospital, only relinquishing the work when he collapsed. An unknown man was discovered at work in the midst of the ruins although his own face was half blown off. Those who escaped with lesser injuries worked day and night while the crisis lasted. Many did not go home for days, so manifold and heavy were the tasks. There was no pause for comment. Conversation was a matter of nods and silent signs, the direction of an index finger. Weeks later the workers were surprised to find themselves aged and thin. The excitement, the stimulus of an overwhelming need had banished all symptoms of fatigue. During the congestion which followed the arrival of the relief trains there were men who spent seventy-two hours with scarcely any rest or sleep. One of the telephone terminal room staff stuck to his post for ninety-two hours, probably the record case of the disaster for endurance under pressure. Magnificent effort, conspicuous enough for special notice was the work of the search parties who, facing bitterest cold and in the midst of blinding storms, continued their work of rescue; and the instance of the business girls who in the same weather worked for many hours with bottles of hot water hung about their waists. An effect which could not escape observation was the strange insensibility to suffering on the part of many of the victims themselves. Men, women and little children endured the crudest operations without experiencing the common effects of pain. They seemed to have been anaesthetized by the general shock. Sidewalk operations, the use of common thread for sutures, the cold-blooded extracting of eyes were carried on often without a tremor. This resistance to suffering was due not only to the increase of energy already described but also to the fact that the prostrating effect of pain is largely relative to the diversion of attention,—as "headaches disappear promptly upon the alarm of fire" and "toothaches vanish at the moment of a burglar's scare." Much pain is due to the super-sensitivity of an area through hyperaemia, or increased blood supply, following concentrated attention. Thus it is actually possible by volition to control the spread of pain, and the therapeutic virtues of an electric shock or a slap in the face are equally demonstrable. This reasoning is also applicable to the absence of sympathetic reactions among many disaster workers. They were found often to be "curiously detached and not greatly moved by the distressing scenes in morgue, in hospital, in the ruins and at the inquiry stations."[84]

Catastrophe and the sudden termination of the normal which ensues become the stimuli of heroism and bring into play the great social virtues of generosity and of kindliness—which, in one of its forms, is mutual aid. The new conditions, perhaps it would be more correct to say, afford the occasion for their release. It is said that battle does to the individual what the developing solution does to the photographic plate,—brings out what is in the man. This may also be said of catastrophe. Every community has its socialized individuals, the dependable, the helpful,

[84] Smith, Stanley K., *The Halifax Horror* (Halifax, 1918), ch. iv, p. 44.

the considerate, as well as the "non-socialized survivors of savagery," who are distributed about the zero point of the social scale. Calamity is the occasion for the discovery of the "presence of extraordinary individuals in a group." The relation of them to a crisis is one of the most important points in the problem of progress.

At Halifax there were encountered many such individuals as well as families who refused assistance that others might be relieved. Individual acts of finest model were written ineffaceably upon the social memory of the inhabitants. There was the case of a child who released with her teeth the clothes which held her mother beneath a pile of debris. A wounded girl saved a large family of children, getting them all out of a broken and burning home. A telegraph operator at the cost of his life stuck to his key, sent a warning message over the line and stopped an incoming train in the nick of time.

Group heroism was no less remarkable. For the flooding of the powder magazine in the naval yard an entire battery volunteered. This was why the second explosion did not actually occur. Freight handlers too, as well as soldiers, revealed themselves possessors of the great spirit. A conspicuous case was that of the longshoremen working on board of a ship laden with explosives. Fully realizing the impending danger, because of the nearness of the burning munitioner, they used what precious minutes of life remained them to protect their own ship's explosives from ignition. A fire did afterwards start upon the ship but a brave captain loosed her from the pier, and himself extinguished the blaze which might soon have repeated in part the devastations already wrought.

No disaster psychology should omit a discussion of the psychology of helpfulness—that self-help to which the best relief workers always appeal, as well as of the mutual aid upon which emergency relief must largely depend. Mutual aid while not a primary social fact is inherent in the association of members of society, as it also "obtains among cells and organs of the vital organism." As it insured survival in the earlier stages of evolution[85] so it reveals itself when survival is again threatened by catastrophe.

The illustrations of mutual aid at Halifax would fill a volume. Not only was it evidenced in the instances of families and friends but also in the realm of business. Cafés served lunches without charge. Drug stores gave out freely of their supplies. Firms released their clerks to swell the army of relief. A noteworthy case of community service was that of the Grocers' Guild announcing that its members would

> fill no orders for outside points during the crisis, that they would coöperate with the relief committee in delivering foodstuffs free of charge to any point in the city, and that their stocks were at the disposal of the committee at the actual cost to them.[86]

By incidents such as these, Halifax gained the appellation of the City of Comrades.

Catastrophe becomes also the excitant for an unparalleled opening of the springs of generosity.[87] Communication has transformed mutual aid into a term

[85] Kropotkin, Prince, *Mutual Aid* (N. Y., 1919), ch. i, p. 14.

[86] Johnstone, *op. cit.*

[87] There is no better evidence of the response of the public heart to a great tragedy

of worldwide significance. As at San Francisco, when from all directions spontaneous gifts were hurried to the stricken city, when in a period of three months seventeen hundred carloads and five steamerloads of relief goods arrived, in addition to millions of cash contributions, so was it at Halifax. So it has always been, as is proven by Chicago, Dayton, Chelsea as well as by numbers of other instances. The public heart responds with instantaneous and passionate sympathy. Halifax specials were on every railroad. Ships brought relief by sea. Cities vied with each other in their responses. Every hour brought telegraphed assistance from governments and organizations. In about fifteen weeks approximately eight millions had been received, aside from the Federal grant. But it was not the totality of the gifts, but the number of the givers which gives point to our study. So many rushed with their donations to the Calvin Austin before she sailed from Boston on her errand of relief that "the police reserves were called out to preserve order." A great mass of the contributions involved much personal sacrifice upon the part of the contributors, as accompanying letters testified. It could be written of Halifax as it was of San Francisco that:

> all the fountains of good fellowship, of generosity, of sympathy, of good cheer, pluck and determination have been opened wide by the common downfall. The spirit of all is a marvelous revelation of the good and fine in humanity, intermittent or dormant under ordinary conditions, but dominant and all pervading in the shadow of disaster.[88]

Abridged and sketchy as the foregoing necessarily is, it is perhaps full enough to have at least outlined the social phenomena of the major sort which a great disaster presents. These are found to be either abnormal and handicapping, such as, emotional parturition; or stimulative and promotive, such as the dynamogenic reactions. In propositional form it may be stated that catastrophe is attended by phenomena of social psychology, which may either retard or promote social organization.

In addition this chapter has discussed the rôle of catastrophe in stimulating community service, in presenting models of altruistic conduct, in translating energy into action, in defending law and order, and in bringing into play the great social virtues of generosity, sympathy and mutual aid.

---

than the fact that at Halifax upwards of a thousand offers were received for the adoption of the orphaned children.

[88] Bicknell, Ernest P., "In the Thick of the Relief Work at San Francisco," *Charities and the Commons*, vol. xvi (June, 1906), p. 299.

CHAPTER III

CATASTROPHE AND SOCIAL ORGANIZATION

The organization of relief—The disaster protocracy—The transition from chaos through leadership—Vital place of communication—Utility of association—Imitation—Social pressure—Consciousness of kind—Discussion—Circumstantial pressure—Climate—Geographic determinants—Classification of factors.

We have seen something of the disintegration which followed what has been called the "stun of the explosion." It included the abrupt flight from, and the emptying of, all the houses and centers of employment, the division of families in the haste of the running and the rescue, and the utter helplessness of thousands in the three basic necessities of life—food, raiment and a roof. There was the dislocation of transportation, the disorganization of business, and the problem of unemployment aggravated because not only was the work gone, but also with it the will to work.

Social organization comes next in order and because its process was associated with the organization of relief—the first social activity—the sociological factors observed in the latter call for descriptive treatment. When the human organism receives an accident to one of its parts, automatic relief processes from within spring at once into being, and it is so with the body politic. This "*vis medicatrix naturae*" assumes sovereign power over all the resources of the community. That part of the social sensorium which is most closely organized in normal hours, first recovers consciousness in disaster. In the case of Halifax it was the army. So was it in San Francisco, and in Chelsea. The army has the intensive concentration, the discipline, the organization and often the resource of supplies instantly available. Its training is of the kind for the endurance of shock.[89] It so happened that at Halifax large numbers of men in uniform were stationed where they could quickly respond to call. They were very soon under orders. The military authorities realized before midday, the part which the army should play. The firemen too were a social group which largely remained organized, and responded to the general alarm soon after the explosion. Their chief and deputy-chief had been instantly killed so they were leaderless, until one of the city controllers assumed command, and in spite of the wild exodus when the alarm of a second explosion spread, these men remained at their posts.

Play actors also display similar traits of collective behavior. They are accus-

[89] What has been said of soldiers is of course equally true of sailors.

tomed to think quickly, to live in restricted spaces, and to meet emergencies. Than the stage there is no better school. Each actor does his or her part and it alone. The Academy Stock Company, forsaking the school of Thespis for that of Esculapius, organized the first relief station established at Halifax. This was in operation about noon on the day of the disaster.

Thus it came about that the soldiers, firemen and play actors may be called the disaster protocracy.[90] They were "the alert and effective," the most promptly reacting units in emergency. And it would appear that the part of society which is most closely organized and disciplined in normal periods first recovers social consciousness in disaster.

It is the events of the first few hours which are of special interest to the sociologist. The word most descriptive of the first observable phenomenon was leadership. The soldiers were foremost in the work of rescue, of warning, of protection, of transportation and of food distribution. But the earliest leadership that could be called social, arising from the public itself, was that on the part of those who had no family ties, much of the earliest work being done by visitors in the city. The others as a rule ran first to their homes to discover if their own families were in danger. From this body in a short while however many came forward to join in the activities of relief.

As already said those with no social, family or property ties were among the first to begin relief work. But many of these started early simply because they were present where need arose. Many indeed of the uninjured folk at a distance seemed unable to realize the terribleness of the immediate need in the stricken area. In fact, owing to the collapse of communication they did not for an appreciable time discover that there was an area more stricken than their own, and devoted themselves to cleaning up glass and the like. But within a quarter of an hour a hospital ship had sent ashore two landing parties with surgeons and emergency kits. With almost equal dispatch the passengers of an incoming train—the railroad terminal at the time being in the north end of the city—were on hand, and were among the earliest first-aid workers. One, a Montreal man, was known individually to have rendered first aid to at least a half hundred of the wounded.

It was early afternoon, perhaps five hours after the catastrophe, when a semblance of coöperative action in rescue work began. Previous to this the work had been done in a rapid and random fashion, a single ruin being dug through a second or even a third time. Then came the recognition of the utility of association.[91] Thereafter the searchers became parties each of which was detailed to go over a definite area. When a particular section had been covered it was so recorded. This process considerably expedited the work in hand. Meanwhile relief was organized in other important directions.

The vital place of communication in society was recognized at once. It is a major influence in association, and upon it in disaster depends the immediacy as well as the adequacy of relief. Connections had been cut by the explosion and the

[90] Giddings, Franklin H., "Pluralistic Behaviour," *American Journal of Sociology,* vol. xxv, no. 4 (Jan., 1920), p. 539.

[91] Tenney, Alvan A., Unpublished lectures on Social Organization.

outside world could only wait and wonder. How little real information filtered through is shown by the fact that at Truro, only sixty-two miles distant, the announcement was made three hours after the explosion that the death roll would not bear more than fifty names. Nevertheless within an hour after the explosion a telegraph company had a single line established, and with news of the disaster, communities everywhere took up the rôle of the Samaritan.

While the great hegira was in progress another leader, a railroad official, drove rapidly out the Bedford Road and commandeered the first unbroken wire to Moncton. Thereafter all that the government railroad equipment could do was at the community's service. Meanwhile the dislocated railroad yards were being combed for a live engine and coaches in commission. A hospital train was put together and in less than four hours after the explosion a large number of injured people were being transported to Truro.

Even before the rushing of the wounded to the hospitals a few began to realize the great human needs which would soon be manifest among the concourse of thousands who waited in helpless suspense upon the Common and the hill. Here they were *en masse*, a typical social aggregation, responding to the primitive, gregarious instinct of the herd. "Like sheep they had flocked together too bewildered for consecutive thought."[92] Yet here ministrations of one sort or another came into spontaneous operation. Soon the military began raising white tents upon the field. One after another they rose, presenting the appearance of an huge encampment. The idea spread by imitation,[93] the repetition of a model,—"the imitative response of many minds to the suggestive invention of one." One or two here and one or two there began to prepare the big church halls and other roomy institutional buildings for occupancy. Hastily the windows were patched up, the glass swept out, and no sooner had the danger of a second explosion passed, and the rumor of a possible roof reached the homeless, than they began to repair thither. At first each improvised shelter became a miniature clothing and food depot as well as a habitation. Then the idea spread of taking the refugees into such private homes as had fared less badly. Imitation is the foundation of custom. It became the thing to do. The thing to do is social pressure. It may be unwilled and unintended but it is inexorable. It worked effectively upon all who had an unused room. Many sheltered upwards of a dozen for weeks; some, more.

In the homes and shelters association of the like-minded soon came about through consciousness of kind. At first it was a very general consciousness which seemed to draw all together into a fellowship of suffering as victims of a common calamity. There was neither male nor female, just nor unjust, bond nor free. Men, women and little children lay side by side in the large sleeping rooms and "shared each other's woes," for "the consciousness of kind allays fear and engenders comradeship."[94] Then followed requests for changes of location in the dormitories, and for changes of seats at the dining tables. As various shelters sprang up, the

---

[92] Bell, McKelvie, *A Romance of the Halifax Disaster* (Halifax, 1918).

[93] Tarde, Gabriel, *Les lois de l'imitation* (N. Y., 1903), translation by E. C. Parsons, ch. i, p. 14.

[94] Giddings, *op. cit.*, p. 396.

religious element appeared. Applications came for transfers from Roman Catholic institutions to Protestant stations and *vice versa*. Even the politically congenial were only too ready to segregate when occasion offered.

Discussion and agreement must precede all wise concerted volition. There must be "common discussion of common action."[95] Propositions must be "put forth" and talked over. There must be a "meeting of minds" and a "show of hands," and decisions made. There had been no preparedness. The city possessed not even a paper organization for such a contingency as a sudden disaster; so that during the most precious hours citizens and civic officials had to consult and map out a program as best the circumstances allowed. It was late afternoon on the day of the disaster when a tentative plan had been formulated in the City Hall. The newly formed committees could do but little until the following dawn.

Men at best are largely creatures of circumstance. Innumerable causes, small and great, conspire to incite social action. But in catastrophe the control of circumstantial pressure[96] becomes almost sovereign in extent. The conditions it brings about, while often delaying measures of individual relief, account very largely for the rapidity of organization. While they limit they also provoke effort. The common danger constrains great numbers to "overlook many differences, to minimize many of their antagonisms and to combine their efforts." At Halifax the pressure of indescribable suffering precipitated the medical and hospital arrangements which were the earliest forms of communal service. But it was the meteorological conditions which commanded the most prompt attention to the consideration of shelter and clothing. The months appeared to have lost station and February to have come out of season. The following table gives the weather record for the seven days which followed the catastrophe.[97] It is the record of a succession of snow, wind, cold and blizzard.

Thursday, Dec. 6th.	9 a. m. Fair. Frozen ground. Light N. W. wind. No precipitation. Temperature: max. 39.2, min. 16.8.
Friday, Dec. 7th.	9 a. m. N. E. wind, velocity 19. Snow falling. At noon N. W. gale. Afternoon, blizzard conditions. 9 p. m. N. W. wind, velocity 34. Precipitation 16.0 in. snow. Temperature: max. 32.2, min. 24.8.
Saturday, Dec. 8th.	9 a. m. N. W. wind, velocity 20. Intermittent sunshine. 9 p. m. N. W. wind, velocity 11. Precipitation 1.2 snow (in a. m.). Temperature: max. 29.8, min. 15.
Sunday, Dec. 9th.	9 a. m. S. E. gale, velocity 39. Streets icy and almost impassable. 9 p. m. S. W. wind, velocity 27. Precipitation .99 rainfall (1.40 a. m. till noon). Temperature: max. 50.41, min. 14.6.

[95] Bagehot, Walter, *Physics and Politics* (N. Y., 1884), p. 159, *et seq.*

[96] Giddings, *op. cit.*, p. 390.

[97] From information kindly supplied by D. L. Hutchinson, director of the St. John (N. B.) observatory, and F. B. Ronnan, Halifax Station.

Monday, Dec. 10th.	9 a. m. S. W. wind, velocity 11. Afternoon, blizzard (worst in years). Knee-deep drifts. 9 p. m. W. wind, velocity 20. Precipitation 5.6 snowfall (2 p. m. till 5.40 p. m.). Temperature: max. 34.2, min. 16.8.
Tuesday, Dec. 11th.	9 a. m. Clear. W. wind, velocity 18. 9 p. m. W. wind, velocity 11. No precipitation. Temperature: max. 18.2, min. 6.6.
Wednesday, Dec. 12th.	9 a. m. N. W. wind, velocity, 15. 9 p. m. N. E. wind, velocity 3. No precipitation. Temperature: max. 17, min. 2.

In consequence of otherwise unendurable conditions, the most rapid repairs were made to all habitable houses or those possible of being made so. The same was true of public buildings, hospitals, factories and warehouses. Moreover the same explanation accounts for the exodus of many who sought for shelter to the countryside nearby; and the many more who accepted the invitation of, and entrained for various Nova Scotian towns which became veritable "cities of refuge" to hundreds. The climate[98] decided the question of reconstruction in favor of temporary structures; for it was a time of year when prompt rebuilding was out of the question. Climatic conditions also seriously delayed the arrival of relief supplies, allowed but scanty provision for many, kept some from the depots of relief, or from surgical aid; and others standing in line in the bitter cold. It also added seriously to the sanitation and shelter problem. But it speeded and spurred the workers to prevent the maximum of exposure and neglect. It called imperatively for the most effective system, and many of the workable methods were hit upon under the stress of storm. An illustration of this may be found in the adoption of many food depots instead of one central station. Regional influence thus "fixes the possibilities of organization and collective effectiveness."[99] The sociologist must study maps of lands and plans of cities. The location of the food stations at Halifax was a matter of topography as were the later administration districts. The city is widely spread out. It has fifty more miles of street than a city of similar population in a neighboring province. Six depots were established for the public distribution of supplies,[100] situated so as to touch the entire needy population most effectively, and to equalize the groups to some degree. So too, in the matter of dressing stations, accessibility was a deciding factor. But even this system had to be supplemented. Bread vans were driven hither and thither and when halted in the center of a street were usually immediately surrounded. Thus social reorganization in catastrophe witnesses to an urgency resident no less in space than in time and reëmphasizes the importance placed upon the physical factors in sociology.

Thus may be said to have come about the transition from chaos to a semblance of community organization. Not the normal civil social order of pre-disaster days, but the establishment of a species of collective behavior, and the organization of relationships apparently of a quite different character. The difference was one

[98] Semple, Ellen, *Influences of Geographic Environment* (N. Y., 1911), p. 607, *et seq.*

[99] Giddings, *op. cit.*, p. 389.

[100] For a period of two weeks meals for 15,000 people were distributed every day.

which might be compared to that between a great relief camp and a city. But the difference was only superficial. Fundamentally there were to be seen the factors underlying all social organization. These have been already illustrated, and are classified as psychological, such as leadership, gregarious instinct, imitation, consciousness of kind, discussion, recognition of utility of association and custom; and as physical, including climate and topography.[101] The conclusion was drawn that the part of society which is most closely organized and disciplined in normality, first recovers consciousness in catastrophe, and the value of a militia organization in every community is a practical corollary. This follows not only because of the imperturbability and the promptitude of reaction, of an army in crisis, but also because of the rapidity with which it can be mobilized, its value in preserving law and order, its authoritative control and power to punish, and because of the attending psychological effects of orderly bearing and coolness in a time of general chaos, bespeaking a care that is at once paternal and sympathetic.

[101] Other sociological factors might also be illustrated, namely, (a) the biological, including, besides the density of population, the heredity and the physical and mental health of the inhabitants. (b) the equipmental factor, including available economic resources, general enlightenment, social surplus and institutional facilities for re-education, *etc.* (*Vide* ch. vii.)

CHAPTER IV

CATASTROPHE AND SOCIAL ORGANIZATION (CONT'D)

The reorganization of the civil social order—Division of labor—Resumption of normal activities—State and voluntary associations—Order of reëstablishment—Effects of environmental change—The play of imitation—The stimulus of lookers-on—Social conservation.

It is not necessary to repeat the fact, which the reader has already seen, that the process of complete social organization was largely expedited by the organization of relief, and materially reacted upon by it. The community's "big men," the men of prominence, the men of broad experience in civic and philanthropic work, the men who knew the resources of the city and had the prestige to command them, were deeply immersed in the relief work while the businesses and the departments of the shattered body politic waited or went forward in a more or less indifferent way.

But this could be both economically and socially of a temporary nature only. "Business and industry must be set agoing. Church and school must resume the ordinary routine. One by one the broken threads of the former everyday life, the life of custom and habit must be reconnected." The division of social labor[102] is a law of society. It is traceable back to the primitive household itself, and is a result of underlying differences. The great "cause which determines the manner by which work is divided is diversity of capacity." With the advent of the social specialists at Halifax a major division of function began. The responsibility for the relief work having been delegated to a special social group, public thought and public men were free to turn their energies to the restoration of a normal society.

But it was the reorganization rather than the organization of relations which the sociologist observes to have first taken place. The stage was all laid. It was necessary only for the actors in the drama to resume their places. The old "parts" awaited them, although many of the "properties" were no more. Or to use the more sociological jargon one might say, there was still the homogeneity of stock, still a dominating like-mindedness, still a protocracy, still a group of mores to serve as media of social self-control. Indeed most of the former complexities of social structure remained. But this was only potentially true. The social relations

[102] Durkheim, Émile, *De la division du travail social* (Paris, 1893).

based upon the underlying factors had to be resumed. Moreover the resumption was accompanied by various changes the significance of which will appear in later discussion. The order of the resumption of normal activities is of unusual social interest as are also the influences which were in play and the changes which ensued. It may be objected that such a tabulation is unfair to the various socially component groups and that the special exigencies of each preclude comparison. But at least one index of the bent of the social mind is the separation of those activities which must needs be first rehabilitated, from those which can wait. Organizing genius was not entirely occupied with relief in the ordinary sense of the term.

Economic vigor is one of the most vital things in a community's life. It is in a sense fundamental not only to happiness and general well-being but accompanies and conditions the cultural institutions, religious, educational and aesthetic. It is not surprising then that commercial activity was in actual fact the earliest aspect of life to resume a semblance of normality. Naturally public utilities were first on the list, for these include systems of communication without which society can hardly be. Reference has already been made to the speed with which a makeshift service was established, but our purpose here is to record the resumption of normal activity.

Wire communication is led out from the city by pole lines. Many of these had been demolished, or broken at the crossbeam. Clerks had been injured and instruments damaged. In spite of these odds one was reconnected within an hour, and by the evening of the day of the disaster six direct multiplex wires to Montreal, three to St. John and one each to Boston and New York, had been established. Upwards of a thousand messages an hour went forth the first week. The work became normal about December twentieth.

The telephone system suffered the loss of the entire northern exchange and of the harbor cable—broken through ships dragging anchor—a total material damage of one hundred thousand dollars. Its personnel was also depleted. Nevertheless telephone business may be said to have been generally resumed on the seventh, the day after the disaster, and the load of local traffic soon attained over one hundred and twenty percent above its average figure. Telephone service was absolutely suspended for only about two hours,—the period of prohibition from buildings,—and the cable telephone for about three days. Messages of a social character were tabooed for several weeks, when the work again became normal.

The illumination service was quickly restored. The company was able to give partial light and some service from noon on the sixth. Periods of intermittent darkness however, were not unusual. Gas service was off until December the ninth—the top of the gasometer having been broken and two hundred thousand cubic feet deflected from the mains into the air—when repairs were completed and on the tenth the service resumed. On the fourteenth gas and electric light service became normal.

Railroad communication had been dislocated. The explosion occurred in the vicinity of the principal sidings and vital portions of the system. Three miles of the main road were buried in debris, the station wrecked, equipment damaged, and crews scattered searching for their dead. In spite of this, as already noted, a hospital train was sent out in the early afternoon of the disaster day and incoming trains were switched to their new tracks leading to the south end terminal. On the evening of the day following the disaster—Friday—the first regular train for Montreal left the city. Two days later the main lines were clear and the first train left the old passenger station on Saturday evening. By Monday the full passenger service was resumed, to and from the station. Eight days after the catastrophe all branches of the service were working and conditions were fairly normal.

The rolling stock of the street-car system sustained much damage. Some of the employees were injured and others were unavailable. A scant service was restored at noon on December the sixth. By six o'clock of the seventh, tram lines in the north section were able to resume an eight-car service. Then the blizzard came and tied up all lines. It was not until Sunday, December ninth, that it was possible to resume any semblance of car service. On the twenty-second of December, twenty-two cars were operating—twenty-seven is the normal number,—but the shortage of men made it difficult to operate the full number. The service was not entirely normal for some months owing to the severe storms all winter which tied up the lines and caused delays, and to the shortage of men to handle the cars.

The newspaper offices by the employment of hand compositors were able to produce papers on December seventh but in limited editions and of reduced size. This was owing to the dependency of the linotypes upon the gas service which had failed. The normal-size production recommenced in a week's time.[103]

The postal service was completely disorganized and was not restored to any extent until Monday the tenth of December. Owing to the innumerable changes of address, as well as many other reasons, it was weeks before there was a normal and reliable distribution of mails.

The banks were open for business the morning following the catastrophe, just as soon as the doors and windows were put in. Traffic of relief trains coming in affected the ordinary trade for three months, more or less, but principally outside of the city. In the city all business in the banks went on as usual the day after the explosion.

Two instances are selected at random to illustrate the resumption of general business activity. Out of much wreckage and a forty-thousand-dollar loss one company restarted paint and varnish making on January second. A large clothing establishment, had been badly damaged. The factory and all branches of the business were running in five weeks—January tenth. Machines were in operation with shortened staffs at an earlier date.

The regular meetings of the City Council recommenced on December twentieth, and were held regularly from that time on. The Board of Trade rooms were not badly damaged and there was no cessation of work or meetings. The theatres were speedily repaired and resumed business on Friday, December the twenty-eighth. The Citizen's Library was a few weeks closed for the circulation of books, and

[103] In the great Baltimore fire of 1904 the *Baltimore Sun*, by remarkable enterprise was gotten out at Washington, 45 miles distant, and did not miss a single issue.

used in relief service as a food depot, thus ministering to a hunger which is more imperious than that of mind in the hour of catastrophe.

Of the churches several were entirely destroyed. In all cases the edifices were injured, organs disordered and windows shattered. Parishes were in some instances almost wiped out. In a single congregation four hundred and four perished. In another nearly two hundred were killed, the remainder losing their property. In a third, of the one hundred and eight houses represented in the congregation only fourteen were left standing. Hurried efforts were made to safeguard church property, but church services were not generally resumed until the second Sunday.[104] Even then the congregations were small and the worshipping-places were not in all cases churches. Theatres, halls and other buildings housed many a religious gathering. While the restoration of churches waited, clergy and church workers gave themselves unremittingly to the relief of the needy, the succor of the injured and the burial of the dead. Their intimate knowledge of family conditions was of inestimable value in the relief administration. Sunday schools were reassembled as accommodations permitted, but it was many months before the attendances approximated the normal.

The school system was badly disorganized. Three buildings were totally destroyed, and all were rendered uninhabitable for some time. The loss was approximately eight-hundred thousand dollars. The members of the staff were given over to relief committees, registration, nursing and clothing service. Early in March, about three months after the explosion, arrangements were completed whereby nearly all the children in the city could attend classes. The double-session system was introduced to accomplish this. Rooms were necessarily over-crowded and ventilation impaired. By May eighth, fifteen school buildings were in use.[105]

Progress in reopening schools is indicated by the following schedule.

Dec. 10	classes in one institution
Jan. 7	classes in three emergency shelters
Jan. 8	classes in a church hall
Jan. 14	classes in five school buildings
Jan. 17	classes in one institution
Jan. 21	classes in two school buildings
Jan. 22	classes in one school building
Jan. 24	classes in one school building
Feb. 1	classes in one institution
Feb. 25	classes in two school buildings
Mar. 16	classes in one school building

[104] On the first Sunday, December ninth at eleven o'clock Archdeacon Armitage conducted Divine service in St. Paul's Church, and the same afternoon this edifice was used by the congregation of All Saints Cathedral.

[105] Quinn, J. P., *Report of Board of School Commissioners for City of Halifax*, 1918.

Apr. 8 classes in one school building
May 8 classes in one school building
May 20 classes in two portable schools

The community as finally reorganized differed materially from that which had preceded. The picture of the conditions at a considerably later period will be fully presented elsewhere. Here will be noted only a few social effects immediately apparent and due to the temporary environmental conditions.

Owing to the number of men required for reconstruction work the Tramway Company found it very difficult to get a full complement of men back into the service. As a result they took into consideration the advisability of employing women conductors, and finally adopted this plan.

At the time of the explosion a heated election campaign was in progress. Then representative men of both political parties urged their followers to drop the election fight and the election was deferred and later rendered unnecessary by the withdrawal of one of the candidates.

The darkening of the water-front, the shading of windows, and other war-protective measures against the submarine menace, were given little attention for many weeks, and the coming into operation of the Military Service Act was postponed.

The establishment of relief stations, and later, of the temporary relief houses in the central and southern portion of the city brought about a very unusual commingling of classes, as well as a readjustment of membership in schools, parishes and various institutions.

Club life, social life, lodge and society "evenings" were for a considerable period tabooed, because of a general sentiment against enjoyment under the existing conditions as well as to lack of accommodation and of time.

The clamor for arrests, for the fixing of responsibility for the disaster, and for the meting out of punishment was for a long time in evidence, but never received complete satisfaction.

The difficulties of restoration of school attendance repeated the experience of the Cherry disaster, and the Truant Officer had a very strenuous time owing to the fact that so many people had changed their addresses.

A number of "special policemen" were recruited from citizens of all ranks, and this force materially assisted the members of the regular department. Owing to the large influx of workmen following the catastrophe, as well as for other reasons the work of the detectives was greatly increased.[106]

The survivors of two neighboring congregations, although belonging to different denominations, united in erecting a temporary church building—their respective churches having been destroyed—and have since worshipped together—a demonstration of the practicability of church union under circumstantial pressure.

[106] Hanrahan, F., *Report of Chief of Police*, Halifax, 1918.

The display apartments of a furniture concern were utilized as actual living rooms by refugees for a period, while at the same time business was in operation throughout the rest of the establishment.

The necessary functioning of relief activities, seven days in the week, the keeping of stores open on Sundays and the general disorganization of the parishes was reflected for a long period in a changed attitude upon the part of many towards Sabbath observance.

German residents of the city were immediately placed under arrest when the disaster occurred, but all were later given their freedom.

The citizens of Halifax were almost entirely oblivious to the progress of the war and other matters of world interest, for many days after the disaster.

The reversion to the use of candles, oil lamps and lanterns was an interesting temporary effect.

The rapidity of the reorganization, as well as the subsequent expansion, noted later, was largely effected by the social law of imitation already noticed. Many of the conditions affecting the rate of imitation were present. There was a crisis, there was necessity, there was trade and business advantage, social pressure, public demand, shibboleths—"a new Halifax" for example—but above all there was a multitude of models. The extent and scale of the rebuilding program in one area, the civic-improvement plans which accompanied the work in that district, the record time in which relief houses were completed, the marvellous speed at which the demolition companies cleared away the debris acted as models and stimuli to all inhabitants. The process of speeding-up spread like a great contagion, until the most hardened pessimist began to marvel at the recuperation daily enacted before his eyes.

Among the models thus presented may be mentioned that of the rapid establishment of the morgue. This, the largest ever organized in Canada, was fitted up by forty soldiers and mechanics in the brief period of a day and a half. Another instance was that of the American Hospital. "At nine a. m. Bellevue was an officer's mess. By ten p. m. the same day it was a first-class sixty-six bed hospital, stocked with food and medicine and, in charge of Major Giddings;" it expressed a veritable "triumph of organizing ability." In the record time of three months, Messrs. Cavicchi and Pagano, with a maximum strength of nine hundred and fifty men and two hundred and seventy horses working ten hours a day removed every vestige of the debris in the devastated area. Apartments were built at the rate of one an hour. Motor lorries multiplied so rapidly that visitors said there had been an outbreak of "truck fever" in the place.

By the stimulus of models, such as these, fresh vitality and motive were imparted to the members of the community. Halifax became busy as never before. New homes, new stores, new piers, new banks, replaced the old as if by magic. Men worked desperately hard.

An influence which must not be left unrecorded because of its continuity of functioning is that of the stimulus of lookers-on. More than two hundred cities in all parts of the world had contributed to the reconstruction, and citizens of Halifax knew they were not unobserved. Articles, lectures and sermons were telling forth to interested thousands how a city blown to pieces, swept by fire, buried under ice and snow, and deluged by rain, was a city courageous beyond words. During the month of December, five leading periodicals in Canada and twelve in the United States arranged for articles and photographs descriptive of the city's advantages commercial and residential.[107] Halifax became a world-known city. This added still further spur to action. Halifax simply had to make good. She was bonded to the world.

There are two considerations which may appropriately bring this chapter to a close. The first arises naturally from what has been said, namely, that in catastrophe it is only after division of function delegates to a special group the responsibility for relief work that public thought is directed to the resumption of normal society. The second is a practical deduction—that of social conservation. Every community should possess a permanent vigilance committee. There should be an emergency procedure on paper with duties outlined to which pledged men may be immediately drafted. Only in this way can social economy be preserved until the arrival of experienced disaster authorities from a distance.

[107] Saunders, E. A., *Report of Halifax Board of Trade,* 1918.

CHAPTER V

CATASTROPHE AND SOCIAL ECONOMY

The contribution of social service—Its four-fold character—The principles of relief—Rehabilitation—Phases of application—Criticisms—A new principle—Social results—Summary for future guidance.

We have already seen that there are certain determining factors in catastrophe and its social results. There is not only the level of the general capability and culture of the community, its power to meet crises and to readjust itself, the scarcity or plenitude of its resources, but also the presence or absence of "men skilled in dealing with crises."[108] In the past, disaster-stricken communities have had such men or have had them not. The disasters of the future—with the exception of those far remote from civilization—may depend on the presence of such leaders. They will come from near and far. The contribution of social service is the contribution of men skilled in dealing with crises. Relief thus becomes "an incident of progress and a social policy." We are now to notice this further determining factor in catastrophe as it applied itself to Halifax.

During the first week at Halifax not only did each day bring its contribution of relief supplies in the way of food and clothing, but each day brought also men and women of skill and experience in social work to place freely their vision and ability at the service of the community.[109]

The Halifax disaster was one of the first of great extent which has occurred

[108] Thomas, William I., *Source Book of Social Origins* (Chicago, 1909), Introduction, p. 18.

[109] J. H. Falk, an expert in charge of the social welfare work in Winnipeg; Miss Rathburn of Toronto, Mrs. Burrington of the Y. W. C. A., Toronto. Christopher Lanz, under whose guidance the rehabilitation work after the Salem fire was brought to a successful conclusion; Katherine McMahon, Head worker of the Social Service Department of the Boston Dispensary, Lucy Wright, formerly Superintendent for the Mass. Commission for the Blind; Elizabeth Richards Day, Organizer and for many years Head Worker of the Social Service Department of the Boston Dispensary; E. E. Allen, Superintendent of the Perkins Institute for the Blind, C. C. Carstens, Superintendent of the Mass. Society for the Prevention of Cruelty to Children; John F. Moors, president of the Associated Charities of Boston, who was in charge of the Red Cross relief following the Salem and Chelsea fires; William H. Pear, Agent of the Boston Provident Association; J. Prentice Murphy, General Secretary of the Boston Children's Aid Society; A. C. Ratshesky, Vice-chairman of the Public Safety Committee of the State of Massachusetts.

since the principles of relief have been authoritatively written. No other community has experienced their application so fully or so promptly. One of the workers publicly stated that "Halifax was further ahead in relief work in two weeks than Lynn had been in a month." It was said that:

> Never before in any extensive disaster were the essential principles of disaster relief so quickly established as at Halifax. In less than twelve hours from the time the American Unit from Boston arrived, the necessary features of a good working plan were accepted by the local committee.[110]

This was, it is true, sixty hours after the disaster, but nevertheless the advent of the social specialists brought to Halifax that something which was wanting when the citizens, astounded at the magnitude of their task, wondered just how and where to begin. When Mr. Ratshesky[111] of the Public Safety Committee of the State of Massachusetts, came into the room in the City Hall where a dozen or so were gathered in counsel, already overwrought with fatigue, it was the coming of a friend in need. It was soon clear that the new-comers had had unusual experience in dealing with other disasters. At once everyone took new heart. Only nine hours later, the Citizens' Relief Committee was ready, and a working plan adopted; and from it grew up a wonderful system worthy of study by all students of emergency relief. Thus social service broke into the midst of the great calamity not as a mere adjunct to what was already well devised, but as a central and deciding element, justifying its faith by its work, and its presence by its wisdom in grappling with an inexorable need.

Of course there had already been a commendable essay toward the solution of what had to be done. Applications for relief came pouring in two hours after the explosion, and industrious workers had already been dispensing to hundreds. On Friday morning volunteers were early at the City Hall, among them many of the public school teachers. A species of organization had already begun, but under congested and the least favorable conditions. A large number of investigators had gone forth, giving information and relief and bringing back reports of the missing, needy, helpless and injured. The Salvation Army had commenced a program of visits to follow up appeals. Clothing of all kinds was pouring into every station where the refugees were gathered together. The Canadian Red Cross was already active. But with the coming of the American Unit,[112] the transfer of the work to a new headquarters upon their advice, and the adoption of a complete plan of organization,[113] the systematic relief work may be said to have in reality begun.

---

[110] Carstens, C. C., "From the Ashes of Halifax," *Survey*, vol. xxxix, no. 13 (Dec. 28, 1917), p. 361.

[111] With Mr. Ratshesky were Mr. John F. Moors, and Major Giddings.

[112] The Public Safety Committee of Massachusetts and the Boston Unit of the American Red Cross.

[113] The scheme as finally decided upon consisted of a small managing committee with sub-committees in control of food, clothing, shelter, fuel, burial, medical relief, transportation, information, finance and rebuilding.

There was a four-fold contribution made by those experienced in relief and disaster organization. The initial service was the establishment of a policy of centralization of authority and administration into one official relief organization. This policy comprised first the coördination of the relief work into one central relief committee, second the placing of the relief funds from all sources into the hands of one finance committee, third the granting of relief by one central management, all records being cleared through one registration bureau, fourth the giving of emergency relief in food, clothing and other things immediately without waiting for the perfection of the relief organization, and fifth, the appointing of a small managing committee to carry out and interpret the general policy determined upon by the executive committee.

If the first great service rendered was that of centralization, the second was that of effecting coöperation. The latter was only partially successful. There was at first an inevitable overlapping, especially in the matter of visiting, some families being visited and subjected to interview a dozen times. Failing to achieve complete coördination, the central committee endeavored to limit duplication so far as possible. An invitation extended to the Salvation Army about December eleventh, to place their visitors at the disposal of the general staff of visitors was declined and it was not until January first that this organization fully coördinated with the rehabilitation committee. It was about this time also that the Roman Catholic clergy agreed to coöperate in the registration plans. On December eighteenth the School Board gave official coöperation by assigning fifteen school teachers as volunteer visitors under the direction of the rehabilitation committee. Another obstacle to the complete systematization of the relief work was the most generous but independent distribution of clothing and supplies from the Eaton Center, and from the station established by a charitable Boston lady. The Protestant and Roman Catholic clergy, as well as the Salvation Army and other organizations received supplies in bulk and distributed to their constituents often with hasty or inadequate investigation.

There was also at times lack of coöperation among the official committees themselves. Friction and crises arose from time to time, which were only stopped short of scandal. They were the consequence either of assumption of authority upon the part of the under-committees, of ineffectiveness of leadership, or of unfamiliarity with the principles of relief. There were also other problems, some of which it may be useful to note. One of these was the problem of the wisest use of local leaders who knew and could interpret the local point of view and method of doing things. Another that of the absorption of volunteers, many of whom could not be expected to understand the nature of scientific relief service.

A third great contribution of social service was that of education in the principles of disaster relief. It was the problem of getting the idea of social conservation understood and established in a community which had not given the subject any thought, and which was quite unfamiliar with the ideals and purposes in view. This was the cause of much delaying of plans, overlapping in giving relief, and giving without substantial inquiry. It explained also the reason for the abundant criticism which arose. When criticism came there was, consequently, no well-in-formed body of public opinion to which to anchor the committee's work.

Educational effort on this subject may be said to have begun with a masterful presentation of the nature of rehabitation at the meeting of the managing committee six days after the disaster. Here was set forth and illustrated the kind of service required and the desirability of such work was at once recognized and inaugurated. Thus the idea of rehabilitation filtered through to the various departments. Trained leaders imparted it to the untrained volunteers. Church, school and club caught something of its spirit and one of the permanent social results of the disaster remains in the partial socialization of institutions. It was this original absence of socialization, this lack of understanding of the true nature of disaster psychology and of the accepted methods of relief that at first made the community so utterly dependent upon the visiting social workers. It may be safely concluded as a fundamental principle that the self-dependence of a community in adversity is furthered by the socialization of existing institutions.

The principles of disaster relief cover three stages, first, that of the emergency period; second, that of the period of transition; and third, that of rehabilitation. These principles in order of application may be thus briefly summarized:

1. The coördination of all the relief agencies arising, into one central relief service.

2. The directing of relief funds from all sources to one bonded finance committee.

3. The establishment of a temporary committee only, at first,—the more permanent organization to await the counsel of specialists in disaster relief, an early call having been sent for experienced workers.

4. The avoidance of, or the early abolition of mass treatment, *e. g.* bread lines, food depots, *etc.*, as detrimental to a psychology of helpfulness and as calculated to delay a return to self-support.

5. The issuing of orders for supplies on local merchants to follow mass-provisioning.

6. The establishment of a policy of renewable cash grants for short periods until temporary aid is discontinued.

7. Continuance of relief upon a temporary basis until all claimants are registered and the aggregate of available aid ascertained, and the needs, resources and potentialities of self-help studied.

8. An early effort to influence public opinion as to the wisdom of careful policies and critical supervision.

9. The family to be considered the unit of treatment.[114]

10. A substitution of local workers wherever wise, and the use of local leaders

[114] "During the emergency stage of relief the people are dealt with in large groups with little attention to the special needs of individuals ... in the rehabilitation stage the family or the individual becomes the unit of consideration."—(Bicknell, E. P., "Disaster Relief and its Problems," *National Conference of Charities and Corrections*, sess. xxxvi, 1909, p. 12.)

in responsible positions.

11. The publication of a report, including a critical survey of policies and methods employed, and a discriminating record of the social results arising therefrom, the mistakes made and other information of value for future emergencies. This report in justice to contributors to include a financial statement.

The fourth great service rendered was that of the establishment of rehabilitation policies and methods. The work of organizing for rehabilitation, as noted above, did not begin until the sixth day after the disaster. On the eighteenth of December the first chairman was appointed. There followed a developmental period during which little progress was made, save in the familiarizing of committees with the object of rehabilitation. "The object of rehabilitation" says J. Byron Deacon "is to assist families to recover from the dislocation induced by the disaster, and to regain their accustomed social and economic status. Emergency aid takes into account only present needs; rehabilitation looks to future welfare."[115] This was the purpose constantly kept in view. The division of work indicates the nature of the task attempted. The division provided for an advisor, a chief of staff, a supervisor of home visitors, a bureau of application and registration, an emergency department, a department of medical social service and a visitor in children's work. Later a children's sub-committee was included.

There was first the record and registration made and verified of all the sufferers and those in need. Over six thousand names of registrants resulted. Five districts or divisional areas were arranged for convenience and thoroughness of administration. One of these covered all cases outside of the city itself.[116] In charge of each district was a supervisor, and under the supervisor the various department heads. Trained workers were drawn into the service and their work and that of the volunteer visitors was directed by capable supervisors. The administration of relief was put upon a discriminating "case system."

There were four important phases in which the work developed; the work of general rehabilitation, the medical social work, the children's problem and the problem of the blind.

The general rehabilitation service was carried on with varied success. It secured valuable intelligence for all committees and gradually increased in working power and efficiency. How many were put upon their feet again through its kindly counsel and careful coöperation cannot be estimated or told in figures.

The problem of medical social service is to learn the social condition of the patient, and to relate that knowledge to his medical condition in order that restoration to health and return to normal family and community relationships shall go hand in hand. A division of medical social service became active a week after the disaster, its workers becoming attached to the several emergency hospitals within

[115] Deacon, J. Byron, *Disasters* (N. Y., 1918), ch. v, p. 137.

[116] The town of Dartmouth on the Eastern side of Halifax harbor also suffered very seriously in the explosion. It had its own relief organization under the very capable chairmanship of ex-mayor A. C. Johnstone. The nature of the relief work there did not differ essentially from that in Halifax.

the city itself and those established in nearby towns. It had as well a working relationship with the military and the permanent Halifax hospitals. Three thousand patients were cared for in twelve Halifax hospitals alone. Trained medical social workers interviewed eight hundred. The one question to which they sought an answer was: "How shall these patients be brought back again as fully as possible into normal lives and relationships?" Having obtained an answer as best they could, the effort was made to help and relieve to the fullest extent that service and science made possible.

The contribution of medical social service was two-fold, immediate assistance and education. By the latter service, which represents the more permanent value to the community, very valuable information and guidance was given to the Halifax Medical Society and the children's and nursing interests. The improvements resulting from these efforts cannot fail to make "follow-up" and "after-care" important considerations in the public health and dispensary work of the future.

Immediate assistance was given by the medical social service in six ways:

1. Arranging for clothing and shelter prior to discharge from hospital.
2. Interviews to understand medical social needs.
3. Arranging about eye problems with the committee on the blind, children's problems with the children's committee, family problems with the rehabilitation committee, *etc.*
4. Making a census of the handicapped, and classifying the returns.
5. Placing responsibility for follow-up and after-care.
6. Intensive case work where social problems involved a medical situation.

Dr. M. M. Davis, Jr. Director of the Boston Dispensary, writes of the medical social service as follows:

> It may well be concluded that no organization or "unit" formed to deal with a flood, fire or explosion or disaster, can hereafter be regarded as complete unless in addition to doctors, nurses, relief workers and administrators there is also a due proportion of trained medical social workers. If twelve years ago medical social service received its baptism, Halifax has been its confirmation day.[117]

The children's service was thorough, as it should have been. If the measure of success in disaster relief is the treatment which the children receive, Halifax relief was above reproach. The children's laws of the province are carefully drawn and adequate, the Superintendent of Neglected and Delinquent Children is a man of singular ability and has wide powers. He became chairman of a strong children's committee with which were associated, besides representatives of the children's institutions, two child-welfare workers of high reputation. This committee came in contact with upwards of five hundred families, including more than fifteen

[117] Davis, Michael M., Jr., "Medical Social Service in a Disaster," *Survey*, vol. xxxix, no. 25 (March 23, 1918), p. 675.

hundred children. Their work dealt with the special problems listed below. More permanent supervision was assumed by the Government Commission about five months after the disaster. The modern principle of the widest possible child-placing was encouraged, the effort being to keep children with parents and wherever necessary to subsidize families rather than institutions.

The work of the children's committee consisted of

1. Getting urgent temporary repairs made to existing children's institutions.
2. Investigating cases to ascertain if children were in proper custody and receiving proper care.
3. Procuring necessary articles of clothing, *etc.*, for children.
4. Hunting for "missing" children, identifying "unclaimed" children, and restoring children to their parents.
5. Interviewing hundreds of people who were: (a) hunting for lost children; (b) wishing to adopt homeless children; (c) arranging for the care of children.
6. Attending to a large correspondence, mostly regarding the adoption of children, for which upwards of a thousand applications were received.
7. Arranging for and supervising the transfer of children from hospitals, shelters, *etc.*, the committee in most cases having sent some one to accompany the children.
8. Arranging for temporary maintenance, permanent care, pensions and compensations or allowances for children, including the finding of permanent homes.
9. Locating and referring to the proper agencies a number of wounded children.
10. Getting possession of children unlawfully taken possession of by improper persons.
11. Arranging for the proper guardianship of certain children.[118]

The problem of the blind, was a special feature of the Halifax disaster. Blindness frequently resulted from the blizzard of glass which caused so great a percentage of the wounds. In large proportion the wounded were women who were engaged in their household duties. The rehabilitation of the blind presented problems of care and retraining upon which was concentrated the skill of three superintendents of important institutions for the blind as well as other specialists and workers. The presence in Halifax of a school for the blind with a capable president facilitated greatly an early grappling with the problem. The contributions of the social workers were chiefly of the character already indicated such as that of general medical social service. There were reported on March first, six hundred and thirty-three registrants,[119] but owing to the difficulties of registration this figure

[118] Blois, Ernest H., *Report of Superintendent of Neglected and Delinquent Children* (Halifax, 1918), p. 110.

[119] Fraser, Sir Frederick, *Report of.*

remains inexact.

Rehabilitation "takes into account the feelings as well as the material requirements of the bereaved families." An additional phase for social workers is therefore mortuary service. Here is required an exceedingly delicate ministry for which few are qualified. It includes quiet coöperation in the painful process of identification, a sympathetic care for those who succumb to shock or grief, and helpful direction regarding the necessary steps to be taken, in interment. At Halifax this presented a remarkable opportunity for service, and an experienced Young Women's Christian Association worker from Toronto attended in such capacity.

There is still another secondary phase which must be referred to as not being without social and moral results,—that of relief of animals. For the sheltering of homeless animals, the dressing of wounds, and the humane dispatch of the badly injured, specially designated gifts had been received. This work received the attention of the Society for the Prevention of Cruelty.

It will be useful as reference data to present here the nature of the criticism to which careful supervision gave rise. It was of the most trenchant character, and it centered about the alleged over-emphasis which seemed to be placed on system[120] and detailed investigations inflicted upon persons of whom many were still suffering from deprivation and from shock, and who were unused to the cross-examination methods of expert social diagnosticians. Often the thoroughness of the records seemed to the sufferers to be the more emphasized part of the proceedings. When all classes of people found themselves in need, there were naturally many who deeply resented being treated so palpably as "cases." But theirs was a choice which left but little regard for personal wishes or sensibilities. It is regrettable however to have to say that the cause of social service did not receive in the community the much larger repute which its magnificent work justified, chiefly because the innumerable "typewriters, card catalogues, involved indexes, and multifarious office equipment"[121] were not made less obtrusive. The merest touch of "cold professionalism" soon became fuel for the burning disapproval which spread through the city regarding the methods of relief.[122] Letters to the press gave vent to the indignation of the sufferers. One of the judges of the Supreme Court was as outspoken as anyone. In criticizing the food-distribution system he wrote very plainly of the "overdose of business efficiency and social service pedantry." Why should needy families be required, he asked, to go through a personal visit and reëxamination at the office every week, before receiving a renewal order for food. Such things were not easily understood or explained. It became increasingly felt that such discriminating and tardy administration of provisions was not the will of the innumerable donors who so spontaneously forwarded the generous

[120] The reader may contrast with this the early days of the relief at the Johnstown flood "where two windows were set apart from which clothing and boots were being thrown over the heads of the crowd, and those having the longest arms and the stoutest backs seemed to be getting the most of it"; and where almoners passed through the streets handing "ten dollar bills to everyone whom they met."

[121] Johnstone, Dwight, *The Tragedy of Halifax* (in MS.).

[122] There was however no definite organization of the dissatisfied as actually took place at the Slocum Disaster.

aid. It was not, so the criticism ran, for the committee to detain and delay the needy recipients for the mere sake of preventing duplication and for the sake of the niceties of case records. At a public meeting in Wards Five and Six, it was charged that "too much red tape had been insisted upon by those in charge of the relief and in consequence of this and other objectionable features of management, there had been many cases of hardship and much unnecessary suffering."

As to the justice of this it has been already indicated that criticism was inevitable because there existed no well-grounded body of public opinion to which could be anchored the wisdom of sound and thorough social methods. The passing of time has reënforced the rightness of the course taken, and not a few former critics would now be ready to condemn the methods used as not having been radical enough. Still there was an element of justice in what was said, and social workers of the future when thrown into a similar situation should curtain their machinery a little closer, at least until the community can realize the principles which organization must conserve.

The principle on which rigid procedure is justified is based upon disaster psychology itself, and is the fruit of a long series of trials and errors. On the first few days after disaster the finer sensibilities of human nature appear. Men and women say "others have lost more, we will get on with a minimum of help." About the fifth day when the poignancy of the horrors has passed and the dead are buried, these same people suddenly discover that there are thousands of dollars available. Then another aspect of human nature comes into evidence. Every device is utilized by each to out-distance the other in the scramble. There has not been a single disaster where this state of mind has not shown itself. The way to deal with it without complete records as yet has not been suggested. The only way a committee can protect itself against disgruntled criticism is to know what it is doing. This is the justification of rigid desk procedure. It is a way to detect and to defeat imposture; though it serves also many other purposes. It was not, however, all adverse criticism which developed at Halifax. There were many who were able to see the beneficent purpose behind the careful service, and as months passed on the value of this experienced administration came to be more generally realized. Indeed

> so large a place did the Social Service workers eventually fill in the community that many reëstablished families begged for the continuance of the department's supervision even though its aid was no longer required. No greater testimony to the value of this rehabilitation work could be given.[123]

When on January twenty-first the Federal Relief Commission took charge of the entire system, it may be said that there was a change not only of hands, but of policy as well. The large amounts made available by the Imperial and Dominion governments and by public subscription made it possible to substitute for rehabilitation the principle of modified restitution. This change of policy the government adopted because of the conviction upon the part of the people that they were suffering from the vicissitudes of war, and that full restoration was in law and equity of national obligation. The step is of special social significance for Halifax is the

[123] Johnstone, *op. cit.*

first instance where on any large scale[124] the principle of restitution became the guide, rather than that of rehabilitation. This principle of indemnity

> implies the reinstatement of the beneficiary as nearly as possible into the position from which he was hurled by the calamity which has befallen him. It implies that to the householder shall be given the use of a house, to the mechanic his tools, to the family its household furniture. For the community as a whole it means a speedy restoration of such economical and industrial activities as have been temporarily suspended, the rebuilding of bridges, the reopening of streets, the reëstablishment of banks, business houses, churches, schools. It requires that protection shall be given the defenseless, food and shelter to the homeless, suitable guardianship to the orphan and as nearly as possible normal social and industrial conditions to all.[125]

It must be made clear that while in no case was the Halifax policy denominated restitution, but rather "generous relief," in actual practice a large proportion of claims were verified and paid on a percentage basis of the loss suffered, rather than that of ascertained need. The Commission was granted power to "pay in full all personal property and real estate claims duly established to an amount not exceeding five thousand dollars." And while in case of the larger claims of churches, schools, business properties and manufacturing establishments, and the property of the more prosperous classes, there was a policy of just and adequate relief declared, the agitation continued and continues that "every dollar of loss shall be paid in full."

Of such a policy in disaster relief Deacon writes: "It is not the policy of disaster relief to employ its funds in restoring losses and compensating for death or personal injury." Commenting on this statement John F. Moors says: "It is interesting to note that at Halifax, the latest scene of serious disaster, such full compensation is intended."[126]

What were the social results of this policy? This question is one of no less interest to the community itself than to the student of sociology. It is perhaps too early for adequate examination and comparison with the policy which formerly held sway. While still a vital question there are observers who have grown dubious, if not of restitution certainly of the lump-sum method of restoration.[127] They assert that for many it proved simply a lesson in extravagance and did not safeguard the economic future of the recipients. Unused to carrying all their worldly goods in their vest pockets, these same pockets became empty again with uncommon rapidity. Victrolas, silk shirts and furbelows multiplied. Merchants' trade grew brisk

[124] Both in Chicago and Johnstown many families were placed in a position practically as good as that which they had occupied before. Carnegie once completely reimbursed the sufferers from a bank failure.

[125] Devine, Edward T., *Principles of Relief* (N. Y., 1904), pt. iv, p. 462.

[126] Moors, John F., Book Review, *Survey*, vol. xxxix, no. 17 (Jan. 26, 1918), p. 472.

[127] The courts of small claims devoted ten minutes to each case. The amount awarded was paid on the day the case was heard.

with "explosion money." There seemed to be a temporary exchange of positions by the social classes. The following statement made by one closely associated with social conditions in Halifax and written over two years after the disaster, shows only too well the danger involved in the application of such a principle. After referring to "the spirit of passive criticism directed chiefly against the few who have borne the burden of restoration" the statement continues:

> The individuals who after all make up a community have been blinded to the bigger interests by their own individual material losses, and the idea of material compensation on a dollar for dollar basis. As some of us earlier foresaw, the disaster wrought much moral damage, for which no "claims" were even presented, even by those to whom we might look for special moral teaching in such an experience. In the course of our work we come daily upon evidences of this condition lingering in our midst.

Upon the whole disaster-study inclines to the unwisdom of "the disposition to proceed as though the relief committee were a compensation board or an insurance society, and to indemnify for loss." But as already said it is early to appraise. What in ordinary times might be condemned might conceivably under the abnormal conditions of war be less morally dangerous. The system may have been at fault and not the principle.[128] Partly for reasons connected with the war it was desired to conclude the business with dispatch, and not to set up a banking house or a training school in thrift. There remains also the final test, the residuum of relief, the number of those who will remain permanently upon the charity list of the community. Will it be said of Halifax as formerly of Johnstown, that "probably so large a sum never passed into a community of equal size with so little danger to the personal character of the citizens and so complete an absence of any pauperizing or demoralizing influences?"

The lessons which come out of this experience at Halifax may easily be summarized.

1. The socialization of all communities should be promoted if for no other reason than for protection.

2. More technical methods of coördination are desirable.

3. To display the machinery of organization is unwise.

4. The supervision of voluntary services should be in the hands of one vocationally trained for the purpose.

5. Further consideration is required as to the policy of restitution and its administration.

6. The wisdom should be considered of establishing a secret relief distribution service, such as fraternal societies conduct for those who though in need will not publicly accept assistance.

---

[128] The policy to be pursued in disaster relief cannot yet be finally stated. It may ultimately be found necessary to distinguish between the loss of property socially owned, and that of private ownership.

7. The necessity of using trained searchers for the dead, who will note the precise spot where bodies are recovered, the centralization of all morgue service, the use of metal tags instead of paper, the sterilization and preservation of clothing and effects for purposes of identification, and in addition the development of a morgue social service with training and qualifications of a special character.

8. The complete organization of a social relief reserve with members beforehand definitely assigned to special tasks, with requisite printed supplies in readiness would render the most effective social economy in emergency. This reserve should be trained in the general organization of shelter, food and clothing, in the shaping of a policy of general rehabilitation, in medical social service, in children's work and in the use of volunteers.

To answer the requirements of what could be called in any sense a sociological treatment of the disaster, the foregoing chapter on the contribution of social service could with difficulty be omitted. Social service introduces a relatively new element of leadership and control upon which disaster sufferers of the future may rely and which assures to any community the presence of those who have special skill in dealing with crises. The "relation of the great man to the crisis is indeed one of the most important points in the problem of progress"[129] in catastrophe. The subject also assumes special importance in the development of the thesis itself. No accounting for social changes which may hereafter be enumerated can be accurately undertaken without full consideration of the major influences which were present. Thus by elimination we may be able to better gauge the strength of the factor of catastrophe itself. The place of government and other social factors, however, has yet to be discussed.[130]

[129] Thomas, *op. cit.*, p. 19.

[130] The author regrets that it has been necessary to omit special mention of the many institutions, societies and voluntary agencies, which were actively engaged in the relief work, and to confine the chapter to the principles employed by those mainly responsible for relief and administration.

CHAPTER VI

CATASTROPHE AND SOCIAL LEGISLATION

Governmental agencies in catastrophe—What seems to be expected of governments—What they actually do—Social legislation—A permanent contribution.

We have thus far been tracing certain of the major influences which are brought to bear upon a community when, after having been overtaken by catastrophe, it is settling back into its former habitistic channels,—channels which not even catastrophe can altogether efface. Some of these influences are intra-communal and self-generating, such as the reconstructive impulses already examined. Others are ultra-communal, such as those vigorous social forces which sweep in upon a disaster city with the suddenness of catastrophe itself.

There is a further influence which is of a community yet in a sense not of it alone, but of all communities—government—that institution of society which expresses its will by legislation, a will which may or may not be the will of the community concerned. And because legislative action is responsible action, and precedent-setting action, it is apt to be deliberative action. Perhaps this is especially true of the new and less familiar field of social legislation. While it may be that the latest group to function effectively at Halifax was government, social legislation when forthcoming contributed an important and deciding influence, and was in turn itself enriched by the calamity.

The boundaries of social legislation are still in the making and daily enclosing a wider and wider field. But not all governments are sympathetic with this process. There are two standards of legislation—the one conserves above all things the rights and privileges of the individual, the other considers first the community as a whole. The superiority of the new ideals of legislation rests here, that it is the general interest which is primarily consulted and becomes the norm, rather than the rights of the individual citizen. Progress in legislation includes its extension into all the affairs of life, retaining as much as may be the liberty of the individual while progressively establishing the interests of all.[131] Its evolution is traceable from the first poor laws, all down the long succeeding line of those dealing with education, health, labor and recreation. However much agreement or disagreement there may be and is as to the wisdom of this mutable sphere of ameliorative legislation, changing just as one ideal or the other happens to be in the ascendancy, there is at least no doubt as to the duty of the government to protect and safeguard

[131] Lindsay, Samuel M., Unpublished Lectures on Social Legislation.

its citizens.

> The one duty of the state, that all citizens, except the philosophical anarchists, admit, is the obligation to safeguard the commonwealth by repelling invasion and keeping the domestic peace. To discharge this duty it is necessary to maintain a police force and a militia, and a naval establishment. Such dissent from this proposition as we hear now and then is negligible for practical purposes.[132]

In this duty all governments alike share, be they imperial, federal, provincial or municipal, according to their respective powers.

At Halifax authoritative control following the disaster was not wholly municipal or wholly martial, but rather an admixture of authorities. Policeman and soldier joined hands as agents of general protection. This service government did and did at once.

One of the activities of the disaster relief first taken[133] was that by the Lieutenant-Governor of the Province of Nova Scotia, when he sent to the Chief of Police of Halifax the following order:

> You are hereby authorized to commandeer and make use of any vehicle of any kind that you find necessary for the purpose of removing the injured and the dead of this city.

The service of the police of Halifax was highly commendable. They worked for long periods with little rest to maintain public peace and order. The splendid service of the King's soldiers and sailors has already been considered. They were first and foremost in the work of rescue and of warning. Military orders to vacate the North End district as a precautionary measure followed hard upon the explosion. Military orders permitted the people to return. Within a few hours after the disaster the military established a cordon around the devastated district which no one was allowed to pass without an order, which citizens having business obtained at the City Hall. This was to prevent looting as well as to facilitate the search for the wounded pinned under the debris, and to permit the removal of the bodies of the killed. The burned and devastated area was policed by the military for about two months with the concurrence of civic authority.

But catastrophe calls for much more than protection. It calls for a procedure, a guidance, a paternal care, and it calls for it at once. If we ask whether it be the function of government to take the foremost step of leadership in this care, the question is one for Political Science. If we ask the more sociological question whether governments actually and always do so, the answer is unhesitatingly—they do not. Says Cooley: "Like other phases of organization, government is merely one way of doing things, fitted by its character for doing some things, and unfitted for doing others."[134] This proved one of the things for which it was unfitted. Not

[132] Giddings, Franklin H., *The Responsible State* (N. Y., 1918), ch. iv, p. 81.

[133] Reference has already been made to the good work of the Government railroad officials in the quick restoration of service.

[134] Cooley, Charles H., *Social Organization* (N. Y., 1912), ch. xxxv, p. 403.

one of the governmental authorities, civic, provincial, or federal, at once assumed and held authoritatively and continuously the relief leadership. Indeed it is a peculiar commentary that they were scarcely thought of as likely immediately to do so. It should be said, however, that the Deputy-mayor—the Mayor being absent from the city—was very active personally. While one of the controllers was himself replacing the dead fire-chief, the Deputy-mayor called an emergency meeting of citizens on the morning of the disaster, and another at three in the afternoon to consider what to do. This meeting of citizens was presided over by the Lieutenant-Governor, and at it, as already noticed, a beginning in relief organization was made. The committees, it will be remembered, were afterwards reformed upon a new basis on the advice of the American unit. But no civic resources were pledged to the people as was done at the Chicago fire. No moneys were then or subsequently appropriated. The Board of Health did not assert or assume the leadership in the unprecedented situation. The City Hall was indeed set up as the relief center temporarily, but the advice to remove it elsewhere was not successfully opposed. How little civic authority was retained under the disaster circumstances is evidenced by the following complaint. The Board of Control which was then the legal representative body of the city had no member on the executive committee of the disaster administration. One of these controllers publicly criticised the method of the Citizens' Committee as autocratic. He "almost had to have a page to reach the Committee as representative of the Board of Control." When the cabinet ministers from Ottawa were sitting in session in the legislative council room, and giving a hearing to a representative public gathering, the Mayor entered a complaint that the City Council and Corporation had been ignored by the acting committees. The Citizens' Committee exercised the general control. They were entrusted with the special grants and the civic authorities, Board of Health, police, *etc.*, so far as emergency matters went, coöperated with them. But the various civic officers were not idle. No one was idle at Halifax. They were occupied with the rehabilitation of the various departments at City Hall and with individual programs of relief. What the civic government continued to do officially was rather in the way of providing the stiff formality of proclamation to the carefully weighed suggestions of the Citizens' Committee. Several of these proclamations were issued. Among them was one urging all people excepting those on relief work or upon especially urgent business to stay away from Halifax for two weeks. Another proclamation was a warning to merchants with regard to demanding exorbitant prices. Over the Mayor's signature went out the nation-wide appeal for aid that "a sorely afflicted people should be provided with clothing and food." The subsequent time, thought and help which City Hall contributed is of less sociological importance to this study. It is sufficient if we have faithfully described municipal aid in disaster as falling under the general category of service, rather than direction.[135]

Turning briefly to the provincial and federal spheres of activity in disaster we

[135] This is not to be considered as without exception in catastrophies. A special Citizens' Committee led the operations at the Paterson fire and flood, but at the Chicago fire the City government took immediate and responsible action. This was also the case at Baltimore when the Mayor was the "key to the situation." It should however be added that both at Halifax and Dartmouth the chairmen of the Citizens' Committees were ex-mayors.

note that no special session of the provincial legislature was called, as was done by the Governor of Illinois after the calamity which overtook Chicago in 1871. Yet when the legislature of Nova Scotia convened a fully considered and detailed act was passed incorporating the Halifax Relief Commission, and designating and defining its powers.[136] The several articles defined its establishment as a rehabilitation and reconstruction committee, a town-planning board, as well as its powers of expropriation, its relationship to the city charter, certain parts of which it could amend or repeal; its powers to enforce attendance at its courts and boards; its relationship to the Workmen's Compensation Act and to the insurance problem. Besides, the Commission was also invested with full and adequate discretion regarding schools, churches and business properties.

Some of the disaster legislative powers and procedures are of special interest to social legislation. Among these were the power to repair, rebuild or restore buildings, the power to repair and carry out a town-planning scheme, the power to amend, repeal, alter or add to provisions in the city charter, the automatic assumption of rights of owner to insure to the extent of the amount expended in repair, and the automatic cancellation of workmen's compensation claims. The act incorporating the commission with powers to make investigation, and administer all funds and properties constitutes Chapter VI of the year 1918. The local legislature also passed Chapter XVIII authorizing the provincial loan of one hundred thousand dollars for the benefit of the sufferers; and Chapter XIX authorizing cities, towns and municipalities to contribute for the relief of sufferers.

The action of Premier Borden of Canada for promptitude and wisdom is comparable to that of President Harrison of the United States at the time of the Johnstown flood. The Canadian Premier at the time of the disaster was in Prince Edward Island, an island province lying near Nova Scotia. He at once left for Halifax and arrived the following day. He immediately placed resources from the Federal government at the disposal of the local authorities to assist them in coping with the situation. The third day after the disaster he attended an important meeting regarding the harbor, and strengthened greatly the morale of the city by assuring a complete and rapid restoration of the harbor. Following the Premier came the Minister of Public Works and he too gave much administrative assistance. Then came five members of the Federal Cabinet, each announcing such programs of restoration as to give the community new heart and inspiration. Among these announcements was that of the establishment of a large ship-building plant upon the explosion area. The Canadian government had already as its first act made a grant of one million dollars, toward the sufferers' relief. It was then forcibly urged upon the government that it assume a responsibility towards Halifax such as the British government accepts in "its policy of holding itself responsible for loss and damage by air-raids and explosions." Public opinion seemed to demand that the work of restoration and reparation be undertaken by the government of Canada as a national enterprise. The government while disclaiming all legal liability, acceded to the request. On January twenty-first there was announced the formation of a Federal Halifax Relief Commission to take over the whole work of rehabilitation

[136] *An Act to Incorporate the Halifax Relief Commission*, Halifax, 1918.

and reconstruction,—an announcement which brought a feeling of relief to the already discouraged workers.

Another interesting contrast may be noted in the fact that while the Governor of Ohio appointed the Ohio Flood Commission to receive and administer relief funds and supplies, the Halifax Relief Commission was appointed by the Governor-General of Canada in Council. This was done under the "Enquiries Act of Canada, being Chapter CIV of the Revised Statutes of Canada, 1906, and under the War Measures Act, 1914, being Chapter II of the Acts of Canada for the year 1914." The Federal grant was later increased to five million dollars, and subsequently to eighteen millions.

There should also be here recorded the timely succour afforded by the Imperial Government at Westminster. Following the King's gracious cable of sympathy, the sum of five million dollars was voted by the British Government to the relief of Halifax. The King's words were:

> Most deeply regret to hear of serious explosion at Halifax resulting in great loss of life and property. Please convey to the people of Halifax, where I have spent so many happy times, my true sympathy in this grievous calamity.

Reference has already been made to the policy to which the Commission was committed. This policy may be more exactly stated by an extract from the act incorporating the commission:

> *Whereas*, the said Halifax Relief Commission as heretofore constituted has recommended to the Governor-General of Canada in Council, that reasonable compensation or allowance should be made to persons injured in or by reason of the said disaster and the dependents of persons killed or injured in or by reason of the said disaster and the Governor-General of Canada in Council has been pleased to adopt said recommendation; *etc.*

In the provision of material assistance, the strengthening of morale and the eventual establishment of a Relief Commission, government may be said to have contributed an important and deciding influence in the reorganization of the community of Halifax and its restoration to normal conditions.

Not only must social legislation be acknowledged to have had a very direct determining influence upon whatever picture of the community is subsequently drawn, but social legislation itself was enriched by the catastrophe. The association of catastrophe with progress in social legislation has already been noticed in our introduction, the mass of facts in support of which no writer has yet compiled. In this introduction we noted how on many occasions disasters have been the preceding reagents in effecting legislation of permanent social value. It is instanced that city-planning in America took its rise from the Chicago fire, that the origin of labor legislation is traceable to a calamitous fever at Manchester and that the Titanic disaster precipitated amendment to the Seamen's laws.[137] It has been said

[137] Parkinson, Thomas I., "Problems growing out of the Titanic Disaster," *Proceedings of the Academy of Political Science*, vol. vi, no. 1.

that "the vast machinery of the Public Health Department in England has rapidly grown up in consequence of the cholera visitations in the middle of the last century;"[138] and also that public health work in America practically began with yellow fever epidemics. Writing of mining disasters, J. Byron Deacon says in this connection

> If it can be said that any circumstance attending such disasters is fortunate, it was that they exercised a profound influence upon public opinion, to demand new effort and legislation both for the prevention of industrial accidents and for the more equitable distribution of the burden of individual loss and community relief which they involved.[139]

Again E. A. Ross writes:

> A permanent extension to the administration of the state has often dated from a calamity,—a pestilence, a famine, a murrain, a flood or a tempest—which, paralyzing private efforts has caused application for state aid.[140]

The student of social legislation who reads this book will turn first to this chapter, and ask what permanent legislation will the future associate with so dire a calamity as that suffered at Halifax. It may be said that not only has special disaster legislation of precedent-setting value been enacted serving in a measure to standardize relief legislative procedure, but social legislation of wider application and more general character ensued. And this was along the line which the student of social law should be led to expect.

As calamitous epidemics bring forth regulations of sanitation; as marine disasters foster regulations ensuring greater safety at sea, it might well be expected that a great explosion would bring about regulations controlling the handling of explosives. And this is in reality what has occurred. There were approved on the twenty-fifth day of June, 1919, by the Parliament of Canada, regulations respecting the loading and handling of explosives in harbors, applicable to all public harbors in Canada, to which the provisions of Part XII of the Canada Shipping Act apply; and to all other public harbors insofar as the same are not inconsistent with regulations already or hereafter made applicable.[141] They cover

1. The provision of special areas for berth, for explosives-carriers.
2. Regulations of ship control to be observed in the navigation in harbors of explosives-laden vessels.
3. Regulations to be observed upon vessels carrying explosives.
4. Regulations governing the handling of explosives.

"The enactment of these regulations" writes the Under-Secretary of State for Can-

[138] Ross, Edward A., *Foundations of Sociology* (N. Y., 1905), ch. viii, p. 254.

[139] Deacon, J. Byron, *Disasters* (N. Y., 1918), p. 43.

[140] Ross, *op. cit.*, p. 253.

[141] *Regulations for the Loading and Handling of Explosives in the Harbors of Canada* (Ottawa, June, 1919).

ada[142] "was suggested in large measure by the Halifax disaster." Had these regulations been in effect and observed in Halifax Harbor it is hardly conceivable that the great disaster of 1917 could have occurred.

It should be borne in mind that the recommendation for this general legislation of social utility originated with the Drysdale commission—a board of enquiry appointed by the Federal Government to determine the cause of the disaster and whose judgment, was issued on February fourth, 1918. In Section XIII of this judgment, the following occurs:

> that the regulations governing the traffic in Halifax harbor in force since the war were prepared by competent naval authorities; that such traffic regulations do not specifically deal with the handling of ships laden with explosives, and we recommend that such competent authority forthwith take up and make specific regulations dealing with such subject.

We, therefore, conclude that the function of government in disaster is of primary importance, and that social legislation when forthcoming constitutes an important and deciding influence and is itself in turn enriched by calamity. Brought to the test of comparison with observed facts the statement in the Introduction, that catastrophe is in close association with progress in social legislation receives abundant justification.

[142] In a letter to the author.

CHAPTER VII

CATASTROPHE AND SOCIAL SURPLUS

Mill's explanation of the rapidity with which communities recover from disaster—The case of San Francisco—The case of Halifax—Social surplus—The equipmental factors—Correlation of tragedy in catastrophe with generosity of public response—Catastrophe insurance—A practical step.

John Stuart Mill offers a very interesting explanation

> of what has so often created wonder, the great rapidity with which countries recover from a state of devastation, the disappearance in a short time of all traces of the mischiefs done by earthquakes, floods, hurricanes and the ravages of war.[143]

This *"vis medicatrix naturae"* he explains on an economic principle. All the wealth destroyed was merely the rapid consumption of what had been produced previously, and which would have in due course been consumed anyway. The rapid repairs of disasters mainly depends, he says, on whether the community has been depopulated.

But this is not an all-sufficient explanation, and indeed applies particularly to countries which have not been bereft of the raw materials of industrial machinery. San Francisco recovered exceedingly rapidly from her terrible experience of 1906. Indeed her quick recovery has been called one of the wonders of the age. San Francisco was not depopulated. Her actual losses of life were but four hundred and ninety-eight, and those injured four hundred and fifteen. The loss of life on the other hand was about two thousand in Halifax, a city of fifty thousand population—but one-eighth that of San Francisco—and her list of injured ran into many thousands. And yet the same phenomenon appeared.

There are other factors both social and economic which must not be omitted from an account of the influences of recuperation, namely the equipmental and other factors which produce social surplus. Disaster-stricken communities cannot survive unless their "surplus energy exceeds their needs." They cannot become normal until the social surplus is restored. The social surplus, according to Professor Tenney, is "merely the sum-total of surplus energy existing in the individuals composing a social group, or immediately available to such individuals."[144] It in-

[143] Mill, John Stuart, *Principles of Political Economy* (London, 1917), ch. v, p. 74.

[144] Tenney, Alvan A., "Individual and Social Surplus," *Popular Science Monthly*, vol.

cludes not only "bodily vigor" but "such material goods also as are immediately available for the restoration of depleted bodily vigor." It is not only physiological, as life energy, and social, as conditions of knowledge and institutional facilities, but also socio-economic, as equipment for the maintenance or restoration of physiological and social needs. In catastrophe bodily vigor may have been depleted, and material goods been consumed. No period of recuperation or rapid gain can ensue unless such equipment is in some degree replaced and a balance of social surplus restored. This is the *conditio sine qua non* of recuperation, and of the transition from a pain-economy to a pleasure-economy,[145] after disaster. Certainly the maintenance of the standard of living demands it. The standard of living has been defined as the "mode of activity and scale of comfort which a person has come to regard as indispensable to his happiness and to secure and retain which he is willing to make any reasonable sacrifice." Following Professor Seager's association of the standard of living with population, the reduction of population in catastrophe of a certain character might conceivably operate to automatically heighten the standard of living, just as the growth of population often brings about its fall. But catastrophe often consumes great quantities of material goods and brings about a change in incomes and in occupations.[146] Seager notes that:

> Actual starvation confronts more rarely those belonging to the class of manual workers, but for them also under-nutrition is a possibility which prolonged illness or inability to obtain employment may at any time change into a reality. The narrow margin which their usual earnings provide above the bare necessaries of life, coupled with their lack of accumulated savings, makes them especially liable, when some temporary calamity reduces their incomes, to sink permanently below the line of self-support and self-respect.[147]

It must be remembered that at Halifax while the equipmental damage was stupendous, still the heart of the downtown business section remained sound. The banking district held together, and the dislocation of business machinery was less protracted on that account. To this it is necessary to add how to a very considerable extent the material losses were replaced by communities and countries which not only supplied the city with the material of recuperation but with men and means as well. Were her own workmen killed and injured? Glaziers, drivers, repair men and carpenters came by train-loads bringing their tools, their food and their wages with them. The city's population was increased by thirty-five hundred workmen, twenty-three hundred of whom were registered with the committee at one time. Was her glass destroyed? Eighty acres of transparences came for the temporary repairs and had been placed by January the twenty-first. Were her buildings gone?

lxxxii (Dec., 1912), p. 552.

[145] Patten, Simon N., *Theory of the Social Forces* (Phil., 1896), p. 75.

[146] At San Francisco "after the fire, the proportion of families in the lower income groups was somewhat larger, and the proportion in the higher income groups somewhat smaller than before the fire." (Motley, James M., *San Francisco Relief Survey*, New York, 1913, pt. iv, p. 228.)

[147] Seager, Henry R., *Economics, Briefer Course* (N. Y., 1909), ch. xiii, p. 210.

Seven million, five hundred thousand feet of lumber were soon available to house the homeless. Were her people destitute? Food and clothing were soon stacked high. Were her citizens bankrupt because of losses? Fifty thousand dollars came from Newfoundland, another fifty thousand from New Zealand, one hundred thousand from Quebec, one hundred thousand from Montreal, two hundred and fifty thousand from Australia, five million from Great Britain. In merchandise, clothing and cash a million came from Massachusetts. In about fifteen weeks, aside from the Federal grant, eight millions were contributed. The total contributions from all sources amounted finally to twenty-seven million dollars.

Factors such as these must not be omitted in examining the sociological recuperation of a smitten city. And when the experience of Halifax is set side by side with the related experiences of other cities a conclusion may be drawn that disaster-stricken communities can always count upon public aid, for the reasons which have already been discussed. But there is found to be strongly suggested a correlation between the striking character or magnitude of a disaster and the generosity of the relief response,[148] as there is also with the immediacy of the appeal. "It is not the facts themselves which strike the popular imagination" says Le Bon, "but the way in which they take place."[149] There have been disasters relatively serious, such as the St. Quentin forest fire, where repeated appeals met with astonishingly little response from the people. "A single great accident" continues Le Bon, "will profoundly impress them even though the results be infinitely less disastrous than those of a hundred small accidents put together." It was in recognition of this principle that "it was decided to transfer the residue of the amount contributed [after the Triangle fire] to the contingent fund of the American Red Cross, to be used in disasters, which in their nature do not evoke so quick or generous public response, but where the suffering is as grievous."[150]

Besides the relation of the tragic in catastrophe to generosity and other expressions of sympathy, the experience at Halifax suggests also a relationship between the aid furnished by a contributing community and that community's own previous history in regard to calamity. As an instance may be cited the quick and splendid response which came from St. John and Campbellton, two New Brunswick cities with unforgettable memories of great disasters which they themselves had suffered. It is also not improbable that the study of comparative catastrophe would reveal a correlation between the relative amount of aid given and the distance of those who give. Indeed there are reasons which suggest that the relationship might be written thus: that relief in disaster varies inversely as the square of the cost distance. The association here suggested is given additional plausibility from the fact that attention to certain types of news seems to vary according to this principle, and news notice is no inconsiderable factor in disaster aid.

Enough has been said to make it clear that at the present time, in the absence of any scientific method of socially ameliorating the consequences of catastrophe,

[148] At the time of the tragic Martinique disaster the New York committee received $80,000 more than it could disburse. (Devine, Edward T., *The Principles of Relief*, N. Y., 1904, pt. iv, ch. vii, p. 468.)

[149] Le Bon, Gustave, *The Crowd: A Study of the Popular Mind* (London), ch. iii, p. 79.

[150] Deacon, J. Byron, *Disasters* (N. Y., 1918), ch. v, p. 120.

relief is a fluctuating quantity, and is poorly apportioned from the point of view of need. While such conditions obtain, disasters must inevitably contribute to the inequalities which break the hearts of men. It is alas true, that after all our generosities and philanthropies

> many people lose their normal position in the social and economic scale through earthquakes, tornadoes, floods, droughts, railway wrecks, fires, and the common accidents of industrial life. These accidents naturally have a vast influence over the lives of their victims; for they often render people unfit to struggle along in the rank and file of humanity.[151]

The only socially defensible way of doing is to spread the economic results of these disasters over the entire community in some form of intra-city catastrophe insurance administered by the Federal government. This alone will overcome the irrationality of an inequitable levy upon the more sympathetic, and the fluctuations of disproportionate relief. And even beyond this step is there not the possibility of an international system in which each nation will insure the other? Certainly at Halifax the aid contributed came from many nations and tongues. But while we are discussing what ought to be and eventually will be done, one very practical step remains which may be taken at once. At the Halifax disaster, we have seen that much of the direction and technical leadership, welcome as it was, and saving the situation as it did, yet came from without rather than from within the country. There is no Canadian who will close these pages without asking whether this must always be. May it not be respectfully suggested, as a concluding result of this study, that the Canadian government, take immediate steps to develop a staff of experts, a reserve fund, and stations of relief strategically located in Canada—these stations to have in their keeping left-over war-material, such as tents, stores, and other equipment together with records of available experts who have had experience in disasters and who may be subject to call when emergencies arise.

And now to return to our thesis, and its special enquiry, namely, wherein is the specific functioning of catastrophe in social change? We have thus far concerned ourselves with the major factors of recuperation, intra-social forces, social service, and legislation.

We find it necessary now to add that the socio-economic constitutes a no less important factor. But the effects may not stop with mere recuperation. Suppose a city becomes in a trice more prosperous and progressive than ever. Suppose she begins to grow populous with uncommon rapidity; her bank clearings do not fail but rather increase; her industries rebuild and grow in numbers; new companies come looking for sites as if dimly conscious that expansion is at hand! Suppose a city rises Phoenix-like from the flames, a new and better city, her people more kind, more charitable, more compassionate to little children, more considerate of age! Suppose there come social changes which alter the conservatism and civic habits of many years—changes which foster a spirit of public service, and stimulate civic pride! Then there is clearly some further influence associated with the day of disaster. Perhaps we shall find progress innate in catastrophe itself.

[151] Blackmar and Gillin, *Outlines of Sociology* (N. Y., 1915), pt. iv, ch. v, p. 402.

CHAPTER VIII

CATASTROPHE AND SOCIAL CHANGE

The unchanging Halifax of the years—The causes of social immobility—The new birthday—The indications of change: appearance, expansion of business, population, political action, city-planning, housing, health, education, recreation, community spirit—Carsten's prophecy.

HALIFAX has had her fair proportion of tribute in her time. Kipling has called her "the Warden of the Honor of the North." Pauline Johnston sings of her pride of situation. As Edinburgh, "it is a city of many charms; beautiful for situation, beyond most of the cities of the world; vocal with history beyond most, for at every turn of its streets some voice from the past 'comes sounding through the toon.'" Her public gardens are the envy of all. Her vistas of the sea are without compare. Her Northwest Arm is a veritable joy. Birds sing in her homes. Cheery wood-fires burn brightly in her open grates. No city of her size is more hospitable than she.

But she has always been a city which has never quite entered into her heritage commercially. Situated where by nature she might well be great, she has always been small. Unambitious, wealthy[152] and little jealous of the more rapidly-growing cities, she has prided herself on being a lover of better things. Commerce and industry were things alien[153] and secular. She devoted herself to standards of art, music, learning, religion and the philanthropies. Charitable and philanthropic institutions abounded. She has had her own conservative English ways. She affected homage to "old families," and to that illusory element "social prestige." She welcomed each new knight which the favor of the king conferred, and grew careless of civic prosperity and growth. She had leaned "too long upon the army and the navy" and her citizens had become "anaemic," "lethargic" and standstill; their "indifference" and "inertia" were a commonplace. Halifax had been complacent and academic rather than practical in her outlook upon the world and her general attitude toward life.

Geographically she suffered by her situation on the rim of the continent. She experienced not a little neglect and isolation because she was an undeveloped terminal, and not a junction point. Travellers and commercial men could not visit her *en route* but only by special trip.

[152] Halifax is the wealthiest city per capita in the Dominion of Canada.

[153] For years real estate was marketed "quietly." In fact, real property was in the hands of one or two specialists only.

Again "the government has had altogether too many interests in Halifax for the good of the place." "Government-kept towns" are not as a rule "those which have achieved the greatest prosperity." Halifax as a civil-service headquarters and a government military depot was perhaps open to the charge of being at least "self-satisfied." Valuable acres of non-taxable land have been far from stimulating to civic enterprise.

An historic city too, Halifax fell under the blight of overmuch looking backward, and sociologically the back look has been always recognized as the foe of progress. But she has had a past to be proud of—one which throbs with incident and interest. Born as a military settlement, she has been a garrison city and naval station for more than a hundred and fifty years. She has been called "the stormy petrel among the cities—always to the front in troublous times." She has served and suffered in four hard wars. She has gloried in this wealth of years and storied past. Her traditions have been traditions of royalty, blue blood, dashing officers, church parades, parliamentary ceremonies, fêtes, levées and all the splendor and spirit of old colonial times. A newspaper has published daily items of a generation before, and weekly featured a reverie in the past.[154] Old in her years she remained old in her appearance, old in her ways, and in her loves. She boasted old firms which have kept their jubilees, old churches wherein was cradled the religious life of Canada, an old university with a century of service. Each noon a cannon boomed the mid-day hour, and like a curfew sounded in the night.

Search where one will, it would be difficult to find another city which has more completely exhibited the causes of social immobility as set forth by sociology. For there are, it must be remembered, causes of immobility as well as factors of social change. They may be geographical difficulties, or elements more distinctively social—an over-emphasis of government, discouraging innovation, too great a "volume of suggestion," the drag of "collective customs and beliefs," a "traditionalist educational system," the "inheritance of places and functions" tending to arrest development, "government, law, religion and ceremony, hallowed by age."[155] All these reënforce the conservative tendencies in society and preserve the *status quo*.[156]

---

[154] *The Acadian Recorder*, C. C. Blackadar, editor.

[155] Ross, Edward A., *Foundations of Sociology* (N. Y., 1905), ch. viii, p. 197.

[156] There are other causes of conservatism. A comparative freedom from disasters in the past is one. Halifax has suffered few in her entire history. Indeed the cholera epidemic is the only one of any consequence. She remained one of the last large wooden cities. Her sister city, St. John, was stricken by a disastrous fire and stands to-day safer, more substantial, more progressive in every way.

Again communities are generally conservative in character when a large percentage are property-holding people. It was one of the surprises of the Halifax catastrophe that so large a number of citizens were found to own at least in part the homes they lived in.

There are other questions which the sociologist would ask if it were possible to carry the investigation further. Is the community loath to disturb the existing relations or to resort to extreme means to achieve desired ends? Or is it eager to sweep away the old, to indulge in radical experiment and to try any means that give promise of success? He would study too the distribution of people relative to their interests. Is there a majority of those whose

Diagnosis in detail is not essential here. Up to the time of the disaster Halifax had certainly preserved the *status quo*. We need not labor the how and why. Tourists had returned year after year and found her unaltered. "Dear, dirty old Halifax" they had called her. They had found business as usual,—old unpainted wooden houses on every side, unswept chimneys, an antiquated garbage system and offensive gutters; the best water and the poorest water system an inspector ever examined; the purest air but the most dust-laden in a storm; an obsolete tramway,[157] a "green market," ox-carts on the main streets, crossings ankle-deep with mud, a citizenship given over to late rising. Instead of making the city they had been "letting it happen." The "transient, the good-enough, the cheapest possible" had been the rule of action.

Such has been the unchanging Halifax of the years. But the old order changeth. The spell of the past is broken. A change has come over the spirit of her dreams. There are signs that a new birthday has come. The twenty-first day of June was the old Natal Day, kept each year with punctilious regularity. But Halifax is now just beginning to realize that there was a new nativity, and that it dates from December—that fatal Sixth. "Sad as was the day, it may be the greatest day in the city's history."

Almost instinctively since the disaster Halifax has come to see the sources of her weakness and of her strength. Her geographical position which once meant isolation[158] will henceforth be her best asset. Just as the geographical expansion of Europe made the outposts of the Old World the entrepôts of the New, so the expansion of Canada and of Nova Scotia—the province with the greatest number of natural resources of any in the Dominion—to the newly awakening city appears full of substantial promise. It will be largely hers to handle the water-borne commerce of a great country. Henceforth the ocean will become a link and not a limit. World-over connections are the certainties of the future, bound up inevitably with the economic and social solidarity of nations. Closer to South America than the United States, closer to South Africa than England, closer to Liverpool than New York, Halifax sees and accepts her destiny, forgets the inconvenience and loss she has undergone and the many annoyances of blasting and of digging, that the facilities of her "triple haven" might be multiplied and the march of progress begin. "The new terminals with their impressive passenger station, will not only be an attractive front door for Halifax, but will fit her to be one of the great portals of the Dominion."

---

experiences are narrow and whose interests are few? Or is there a majority of those who have long enjoyed varied experiences and cultivated manifold interests, that yet remain harmonious? He studies the character of the choices, decisions, selections in a people's industry, law-making, educational and religious undertakings. It is thus that he proceeds in diagnosing a population as to the degree of conservatism and to discover what the ideal community should be.—Giddings, Franklin H., *Inductive Sociology* (N. Y., 1909), p. 178, *et seq*.

[157] Halifax has now one of the best equipped tramway systems to be found anywhere. There has recently been appropriated the sum of $200,000 for sewers, $150,000 for water, $300,000 for street paving.

[158] Halifax long felt herself to have been commercially a martyr to Confederation.

There has come upon the city a strange impatience of unbuilt spaces and untaxed areas sacred for decades to military barracks and parades. She has urged for some immediate solution, with the result that military property will be concentrated and many acres released to the city for its own disposal.

Whether the pendulum will swing so far as to imperil the retention of old historic buildings, time-stained walls, and century-old church-yards is not yet apparent; although suggestions have been made which would have astounded the Halifax of a generation ago. Certain it is that a period of orientation is at hand. There is a stirring in the wards and clubs for progressive administration and modern policies. "Here as elsewhere the time has now come for clear thinking and the rearrangement of traditional thought."

Indications of change are already abundant. The first to note is that of appearance. For illustration may be quoted an editorial published near the second anniversary of the explosion:

> Halifax has been improving in appearance since the explosion, exhibiting very sudden changes at particular points. One almost forgets what the city was like about ten years ago. Still there is a great deal to be done in the way of improvement to our streets. The move in the direction of permanent streets is an excellent one and if carried out as designed will be an improvement and saving to the city.

The report of the Secretary of the Board of Trade makes the following reference to the change in appearance of the city:

> One of the pleasing features in reference to both the wholesale and retail business of Halifax is the improved condition of premises over a few years ago; retail stores are now having up-to-date and attractive fronts, while wholesalers are improving their show-rooms and thereby increasing their sales.

The Mayor writes regarding the sidewalk improvement:

> Some twenty miles of concrete sidewalks to be constructed are on the order paper to be taken in turn so as to be as uniform as possible. This will go a long way toward improving the appearance of the city.

As to the change in the style of houses the Mayor states:

> A pleasing feature of the new construction is the departure from the former square box style of dwelling, also the method of placing rows of houses exactly in the same style. Today homelike houses of modern design, set back from the street with lawns in front are the order of the day—bungalows are particularly in favor.

Fine new residences are being built, apartment ideas are spreading, new lights are being tried out, a new tram company has taken hold. Indeed one citizen is credited with the words: "It is almost a sacrilege that Halifax should be so changed."

The consciousness of change is seen in an altered public opinion and the beginnings of a new civic outlook. Evidence of the new note is a statement by one of the progressive Halifax firms:

> Halifax is going to make good. Outside firms are taking up valuable sites in our business districts. The banks are increasing their activities. Some of the biggest industries are coming our way. Surely everything points toward prosperity.

Another feature indicative of the changing consciousness, which has infected a much wider region than Halifax itself is the plan now making rapid progress for an Old Home Summer, to be held from June to October, 1924. The project has already received legislative recognition. An effort will be made to recall former residents on a scale such as has never been attempted before. The committee in charge is made up of many prominent citizens and the "1924 Club" grows. One may observe still another indication of the determination to progress in the recent completion of a system linking-up Halifax by telephone with Montreal, Toronto, New York and Chicago.

Indices of business conditions are far from satisfactory, yet the items used in their computations are the only ones upon which variations may be even roughly gauged. Roger Babson puts as the leading considerations: (1) Building and real estate; (2) bank clearings; (3) business failures. Other symptomatic facts are postal revenues, tramway receipts, exports, taxes, interest rates, insurance, wages and hours, commodity prices, unfilled orders, immigration and unemployment.[159]

With regard to the first the following statement issued by the Mayor is significant. He says:

> The year 1919 has been one of exceptional prosperity in the City of Halifax. It has been a record year for building. Permits to the approximate value of $5,000,000 have been issued to the engineer's office, the largest amount by far in its history, the amount being practically ten times that of 1913, or the year before the Great War commenced. A part of this only can be attributed to the terrible explosion of 1917.

He refers to the great amount of construction going on in the western and northwestern parts of the city which were relatively untouched by the disaster. The Mayor further states:

> It must be remembered that it is only two years since the devastation caused by the explosion and strangers in the city have considered it wonderful that we are so far advanced in building up that portion which only a year ago had not a house upon it.

The following tabulation gives the building figures according to the permits issued at the City Hall. It shows a remarkable recent increase.

[159] Chaddock, Robert E., Unpublished Material.

Building Permits	
1910	$471,140
1911	508,836
1912	589,775
1913	839,635
1914	874,320
1915	1,066,938
1916	1,177,509
1917	844,079
1918	2,955,406
1919	5,194,806

With regard to real estate the Mayor writes in December 1919

> The increase in the selling values of properties is remarkable. Business property has taken a jump in value, and it is difficult to get for business purposes property well situated unless at very high prices. Property has been known to change hands within a year at approximately double the amount originally paid.

The Secretary of the Board of Trade reports:

> Real estate has been active, and prices have been obtained greatly in excess of what properties were valued at in pre-war days.

In the matter of bank clearings[160] the following table indicates a very considerable change:

Bank Clearings	
1910	$95,855,319
1911	87,994,043
1912	100,466,672
1913	105,347,626
1914	100,280,107
1915	104,414,598
1916	125,997,881
1917	151,182,752
1918	216,084,415
1919	241,200,194

As to business failures the Secretary says:

> Business failures have been few—practically the whole

[160] The reader will of course remember the general inflation of currency.

amount of the liabilities will be made up of one failure, and it is believed the loss to creditors in this particular case will be slight.

Additional Indices

	Gross Postal Revenue	*Tramway Receipts (gross)*
1910	$114,318	$477,109
1911	119,561	502,399
1912	132,097	539,853
1913	140,102	605,933
1914	147,943	645,341
1915	154,499	718,840
1916	167,594	559,513
1917	255,815	859,667
1918	305,412	998,702
1919	349,507	1,258,503

Among other assurances at the new prosperity and the beginnings of fresh faith in the city's future is the coming of new large business interests into the city. Among the largest construction work is the building of the Halifax shipyards upon the explosion ground, involving an outlay of ten millions of dollars. There is the ever-extending plant of the Imperial Oil Company, which will eventually make of Halifax a great oil-distribution port. There is the continuation of the thirty-million-dollar scheme of modern terminal facilities, which have been constructed so close to the ocean that a ship may be out of sight of land within an hour after casting off from the quay.

In short there has been, as has been said, an "impetus given to business generally." That the impetus will continue there is every prospect. Halifax may experience a temporary wave of depression when such waves are flowing elsewhere. But today there are fewer doubters and more believers. The day of new elevators, new hotels, harbor-bridges and electric trains is not very far away. The prophecy of Samuel Cunard made in 1840—when he inaugurated the first Trans-Atlantic line—that "Halifax would be the entering port of Canada"—seems destined to fulfilment.

As regards population after disasters Hoffman writes:

> Even an earthquake such as affected the city of San Francisco may not materially change the existing numbers of the population after a sufficient period of time has elapsed for a reassembling of the former units, and a return to the normal conditions of life and growth.[161]

Yet as before remarked, the catastrophe at Halifax eclipsed all preceding disasters to single communities on the Continent of America in the toll of human life.[162]

[161] Hoffman, Frederick L., *Insurance, Science and Economics* (N. Y., 1911), ch. ix, p. 337.

[162] In the Texas flood of 1900 there were lost 5,000 lives, but they cannot be said to

In the San Francisco earthquake the loss was four hundred and ninety-eight; at the Chicago fire three hundred; at the Iroquois theatre fire in the same city, five hundred and seventy-five; at the Chester explosion one hundred and twelve; at the Johnstown flood two thousand. It is now estimated that the disaster at Halifax probably passed this latter figure, decreasing the city's population by four per cent. Notwithstanding this heavy draught upon the population, the 1918 volume of the Halifax Directory contained six hundred and fifty more names than the previous year.

In the light of this consideration the following indication of the growth of population is also of contributory interest.[163]

TABLE

1911	46,619
1912	46,619
1913	47,109
1914	47,109
1915	47,473
1916	50,000
1917	50,000
1918	50,000
1919	55,000
1920[164]	65,000

An index of the growth of practical civic interest upon the part of citizens is revealed by the comparison of the numbers participating in political action by means of the vote. Recent figures for Halifax are:

POLITICAL ACTION

Year	*Purpose*	*Eligible voters*	*No. voting*	*Percentage of Indifference*	*Percentage of Interest*
1918	For Mayor	7,632	2,769	63.80	36.20
1919	For Mayor	8,890	4,264	52.10	47.90
1920	For Mayor	11,435	5,491	51.99	48.01

Instead of the disaster resulting in disheartenment and a gradually diminishing civic interest, the percentage of indifference is smaller and the percentage of interest is larger for 1920 than for 1919, and the percentage of interest for 1919 is larger than that for the previous year. The number of eligible voters also shows increase. "The campaign [for 1920] has marked a new era .... and will make it easier to institute new reforms."[165]

have been all associated with a single community.

[163] Figures kindly supplied by Mr. John H. Barnstead, Registrar, Halifax.

[164] The Directory of 1920 estimates the present population to be 85,000.

[165] Halifax *Morning Chronicle*, April 29, 1920.

Of further sociological interest is the change affecting city-planning, civic improvement, housing, health, education and recreation.

In the realm of city-planning[166] and civic improvement, Halifax is awaking to the importance of taking advantage of an opportunity which comes to a city but seldom save through the avenue of disaster. The present Town-planning Board was formed as a result of the Town-planning Act of 1915. A board of four members, including the city engineer constitute the committee. The limits of the area to be brought under the scheme were still undecided when the explosion came. The disaster "hastened the resolution" of the Board. "When the disaster came it seemed that things would have to come to a head." Mr. Thomas Adams, the Dominion Housing and Town-planning Advisor, was brought to Halifax to help determine what should be done. "The disaster simply had the effect of bringing to a point certain things which were pending at the time. If that event had not occurred we would by this time be into a scheme, though possibly not so far as we are." Today the limits of the area have been defined and the scheme is nearly ready for presentation to the Council for adoption. The Dominion Town-planning Advisor's assistant reports that real progress has been made in the Halifax plan dealing with the proposed zoning of the city into factory, shopping and residential districts, the provision for future streets, street-widening and building lines, and suggestions for park and aerodrome sites. In the devastated area he has remarked progress in street-opening, in grading of the slope and in architectural treatment of the houses. Five hundred trees and three hundred shrubs have been ordered to be planted in this area. The whole area is under the control of the Relief Commission, for the Act appointing the Commission gave it the powers of a Town-planning Board.

The disaster may thus be said not only to have hastened the resolution of the existing committee, but to have produced two planning-boards instead of one. Each must keep in mind the true ideal. For it is not the "City Beautiful" idea, but that of utility that is fundamental to city-planning. It is a principle to reduce to the minimum the social problems of community life, to accomplish Aristotle's ideal—"the welfare and happiness of everyone." In so doing civic beauty will not be neglected. "Scientific, sensible and sane city-planning" says an authority "with utility and public convenience as its primary consideration produces beauty—the beauty that is the result of adapting successfully a thing to its purpose." It is in accordance with this principle of civic art that the terminal area is being developed—a work designed by the same architect who planned the Chateau Laurier and the Ottawa Plaza with such aesthetic taste.

To "deep cuttings, spanned by fine bridges, and bordered with trees and pleasant driveways, after the manner of Paris," and to a "waterfront as stately as Genoa's, a terminal station with a noble facade, overlooking a square and space of

[166] The earliest city-planning was mediaeval. Halifax was laid out by military engineers with narrow streets—the "ideal was a fortified enclosure designed to accommodate the maximum number of inhabitants with the minimum of space." In 1813 a town-planning scheme was set on foot for the purpose of straightening streets, the removal of projections and banks of earth and stones which at that time existed in the center of streets. Considerable betterment resulted but unfortunately many fine trees were cut down.

flowers,"[167] the future will also bring to Halifax

> more street-paving, sidewalks, parks, fountains, hedges, driveways, cluster-lighting, statuary, buildings of majesty, spaciousness and beauty. Wires will be buried, unsightly poles will disappear.... With time will come all these things which stamp a city as modern, as caring for the comfort of its people, their pleasure and rest, and health and safety. All these things come with time, effort, development of city pride, and the concentrated desire of a people for them.[168]

The question of housing is recognized as an old Halifax problem. It was already an acute one when the blow of the catastrophe fell and multiplied the difficulty a thousand-fold. The Relief Commission has grappled with its end of the problem, namely, the housing of the many refugees who were first accommodated in lodgings and in temporary shelters.[169] The old sombre frame-constructed buildings of the pre-disaster days are being replaced with attractive hydrostone. A hard-working wage-earning community is stepping out of indifferent structures into homes both comfortable and well-ordained.

But the old problem would have still remained unsolved, had not the city authorities caught something of the reconstruction spirit and felt the sharp urge of increasing difficulties. Action has been at last precipitated. However, lacking in comprehensiveness the first attempts, the city has bestirred itself and has come to realize adequate housing to be a supreme need of the community and vitally associated with the city's health and welfare. A Housing Committee of five members has been formed, having as chairman a man of widely recognized building experience and as director of housing, a capable citizen. It is intended to make full use of the federal housing scheme, in a practical way, the City Council having reversed its former decisions and accepted by by-law the obligation which the government act requires. It is hoped in this way to promote the erection of modern dwellings and to "contribute to the general health and well-being of the community."

Thus the principle of promotive legislation and government aid, which when finally accepted in 1890, began the remarkable housing reform in England, has entered the City of Halifax, and will eventually write a record of increased health, comfort and contentment. How soon that record is written will largely depend upon the citizens themselves and their response to a leadership that is forceful as well as wise.

The matter of health organization in Halifax affords perhaps the most significant contrast with the pre-disaster days. Prior to the catastrophe public health organization was not a matter for civic pride. The dispensary, which is often re-

[167] MacMechan, Archibald, "Changing Halifax," *Canadian Magazine*, vol. xli, no. 4, pp. 328, 329.

[168] Crowell, H. C., *The Busy East*, vol. x, no. 7, p. 12.

[169] A model housing development of 346 houses in the new north end has followed the disaster. "It is reasonable to assume," writes an observer, "that the standard of living will ascend. Already the influence of these new houses is showing itself in the homes that are springing up all over the city."

garded as the index of a city's care for health, had received scant support and could only perform indifferent service. Adequate sanitary inspection could not be carried out for want of inspectors. The death rate[170] had averaged about twenty percent for a period of ten years, and the infant and tuberculosis mortality had been tremendously high—the former reaching the figure of one hundred and eighty-two.[171] There was no spur to progressive administration. The city was too ill-equipped to cope with such conditions.

Today Halifax has the finest public health program and most complete public health organization in the Dominion. The fact that this is so is in very close relation to the catastrophe inasmuch as an unexpended balance of relief moneys[172] has been redirected by request for health purposes in Halifax. A five-year policy has been inaugurated. Fifty thousand dollars per year of the relief money, fifteen thousand dollars per year of the Canadian government money and five thousand dollars per year each, of the city and provincial money are to be expended in the five-year campaign. The sum totals seventy-five thousand dollars per year, or practically one dollar per capita.

A completely equipped health centre has been established including all the essential remedial and educational agencies, namely, pre-natal, pre-school-age, school-age, tuberculosis, venereal disease, eye, ear, nose and throat clinics. There will also be provision for the growth of health ideas through mother's classes, first-aid, and sanitary leagues. A public health course for nurses is included in the educational campaign.[173] A most successful baby-saving exhibit has been held, and the plan calls for a full-time tuberculosis specialist.

Upon the part of the civic authorities there has been a greater realization of responsibility. Progressive steps have been already taken including the appointment of a Doctor of Public Health, and the provision of district sanitary inspectors. Restaurants and all places where food is exposed for sale are being systematically inspected with a view of effecting improvements. A single instance of commendable activity along sanitary lines is the prohibition of movable lunch cars, which have been seen on the streets of Halifax for years. The removal of a lot of dwellings unfit for occupation is receiving the attention of the officials. In fact it is the intention of the present Council to improve conditions throughout the city generally as quickly as is feasible to do so. Another illustration of the direction of attention to modern social methods is the present discussion of plans for a psychiatric clinic for mental hygiene and the discovery of defectives, especially those attending the schools. Still another indication of interest in child welfare is the fact that a clinic for babies was established in a central locality and a nurse for babies regularly employed. The hitherto meager hospital facilities are being amplified by the building of a maternity hospital and the enlargement of the children's hospital,—a centralization plan of hospital service being a unique and distinctive feature. In the way

[170] London's is 14.6, New York's 13.6.

[171] New York's is 90, New Zealand's 60.

[172] These funds are from the munificent gift of Massachusetts. A Massachusetts-Halifax Health Commission has been formed—Dr. B. Franklin Royer is the executive officer.

[173] Dalhousie University has recently graduated the first class of nurses in Canada to receive the Diploma of Public Health.

of industrial hygiene a full-time nurse is employed in the ship-building plant and here also safety policies have been introduced and have reduced accidents to a minimum. The movement for the control of preventable disease is gaining impetus and a modern tuberculosis hospital is being established. The Victoria General Hospital is being enlarged and extended, the additions having an estimated cost of half a million dollars.

But it is not alone the activities of the Health Commission but also the earlier vigorous policy of disaster medical relief, which is seen reflected in the growing sense of community-responsibility for health conditions. Halifax has come to see the principle fundamental to all health reform, that public health is a purchasable commodity and that improvement in vital statistics is in close correlation with the progress of health organization. It remains to be seen whether so favored a community will also lead the way in the registration and periodic health examination of every individual citizen which is the final goal of all policies of health reform.

The standards of education have always been high in Halifax. She has been the educational center of the Maritime Provinces. Her academic attainments have brought to her much distinction and not a little glory. Her public schools boast many a fine record to furnish inspiration to each successive generation. To secure appointment to the Halifax teaching staff the applicant must possess the highest qualifications. But however much educational leaders may desire them, modern methods and up-to-date equipment await in large measure the public will. Only where there is a will is there a way. That the public will in Halifax is becoming awakened to the vital rôle her educators play is being proven by the response to the campaign for the expansion of Dalhousie University. That response has been most generous and general, while local contributions have been amplified by large benefactions from the Carnegie Corporation and the Rockefeller Foundation. Of the latter benefactions together amounting to one million dollars—four hundred thousand will be expended upon buildings and equipment. The modernizing process is shown again in the decision of the university to establish at once a Faculty of Commerce and to encourage the teaching of Spanish and Portuguese in the educational institutions of the city.

In the old teaching methods all are given the same course of instruction regardless of the individual mental differences. Today the effort is to provide an education to fit the mind rather than to force the mind to fit the education. In the public schools of Halifax there are not lacking indications which herald the coming of the newer pedagogy. Among these may be mentioned the opening of sub-normal classes for retarded children, experimentation with the social-recitation system, the display of Safety-First League posters and the development of those departments already established, *viz.* vocational and domestic training, manual and physical education, medical inspection, supervised playgrounds, school nurses, dental clinics, and the wider use of school plants in evening technical classes.

Halifax will sooner or later decide to employ to the fullest degree all the opportunities which child-training affords. The school system is an institution of society to mediate between a child and his environment. Children must learn to do and to be as well as to know. Their plastic minds must receive practice in resistance to domination by feeling and in the use of the intellect as the servant and guide of life. To the children of Halifax is due eventually a thorough training in citizenship. This is the last call of the new future in education. It rests upon the twin pillars of educational psychology and educational sociology.

Recreation is still another sphere of civic life wherein the City of Halifax has taken a forward step. In making her plans for the future she has not forgotten that the rebuilt city should contain every facility for children to grow up with strong bodies and sane minds; as well as public provision for the leisure time of the adult population. A Recreation Commission has been formed made up of representatives of the various civic bodies and from the civic and provincial governments.[174] A playground expert was called in by the city government, who after study of the situation and conference with local groups, recommended a system of recreation as part of the general city plan. Already marked progress has resulted; indeed it has been said that the "municipal recreation system of Halifax has made a record for itself." A hill of about fifteen acres in the heart of the devastated area has been reserved for a park and playground. The city has built and turned over to the Commission a temporary bath-house, and has set aside the sum of ten thousand dollars for a permanent structure. The plans contain recommendations for minimum play-space for every school child, a central public recreation area, an open-air hillside stadium, as well as a community center with auditorium, community theatre, natatorium, gymnasium, and public baths. The real significance of this movement Halifax has not, herself, as yet fully realized. Just as there is a close relationship between health organization and mortality tables, so there is a close association between open spaces, street play, *etc.*, and juvenile, as well as other forms of delinquency.[175] The moral value of organized recreation was itself demonstrated in the war, while the increasing menace of industrial fatigue, as well as the fact of the shorter working-day, call for public recreational facilities as a social policy. This policy is not however fully carried out with merely constructive and promotive action. It must be followed by restrictive and regulatory control of commercialized recreation, and wise and adequate systems of inspection for amusement in all its forms. This is the path of progress in socialized recreation.

Progress in coöperation has also to be noticed. There has been a new sense of unity in dealing with common problems. The number of things which perforce had to be done together during the catastrophe was great. This doing of things together will be continued. The establishment of the Halifax Coöperative Society is initial evidence of a movement towards coöperative buying. Coöperation for

[174] It should be stated that the supervised playground movement had been developing in Halifax for a period of fourteen years, first under the Women's Council, afterwards under a regularly incorporated association with which the Women's Council merged.

[175] In view of the explosion and the resulting housing conditions, an increase in juvenile delinquency might have been expected, but the "playgrounds which were established immediately after the disaster, and which adjoined both of the large temporary housing projects, are, it is felt, responsible for the excellent conditions which exist. The records of the Superintendent of Neglected and Delinquent Children show that there was an actual decrease in the number of juvenile arrests in 1918 over 1917."—(Leland, Arthur, "Recreation as a Part of the City Plan for Halifax, N. S., Canada," *Playground*, vol. xiii, no. 10, p. 493.)

community ends even now is revealing itself in the new interest for the common control of recreation, health conditions, *etc.* "The disaster," runs an article in the press, "has given our social movement an impetus. The social workers of the different creeds and classes have discovered each other and are getting together."[176] The organization of social service which only a few years back took a beginning in the form of an unpretentious bureau has shot ahead with amazing rapidity and now exercises an influence of coördination upon the churches, charities and philanthropic societies of the city.

The unifying process is well illustrated by the increased coöperation upon the part of the churches. Following the disaster the churches of the city united into a single organization for relief service under the chairmanship of the Archbishop of Nova Scotia. Since then a Ministerial Association has been formed which has directed coöperative effort along various lines and has exercised pressure upon those in authority where the best interests of the city were involved.

Thus the City of Halifax has been galvanized into life through the testing experience of a great catastrophe. She has undergone a civic transformation, such as could hardly otherwise have happened in fifty years. She has caught the spirit of the social age. This spirit after all means only that the community is just a family on a larger scale, and the interests of each member are interwoven with those of all. But merely to catch the spirit will not suffice. It must be cherished through an inevitable period of reaction and passivity, and then carried on still further into the relations of capital and labor, into the realm of socialized recreation and into those multiform spheres of social insurance whither all true social policies lead.

All these converging lines taken not singly but together constitute a very real basis of faith in the city's future, and of hope for permanent changes for the better. Perhaps this attitude cannot be more fittingly expressed than in the words of Carstens:

> The Halifax disaster will leave a permanent mark upon the city for at least a generation, because so many of the living have been blinded or maimed for life. But it is possible that the disaster may leave a mark of another sort, for it is confidently believed by those who took part in the relief work during the first few weeks that Halifax will gain as well as lose. The sturdy qualities of its citizens will bring 'beauty out of ashes.'

But it is rather for social than for material progress that the sociologist will seek and Carstens continues:

> It may reasonably be expected that through this Calvary, there may be developed a program for the care, training and education of the sightless as good if not better than any now existing, that medical social service will be permanently grafted upon the hospital and out-patient service of the community, and that the staff of teachers of the stricken city, by direct contact with the intimate problems of the families of the children they have in their

[176] Halifax *Evening Mail*, March 22, 1918.

class-rooms may acquire a broader view of their work. If there should result no other benefits, and there are likely to be many, as for example city-planning, housing and health, the death and suffering at Halifax will not have been in vain, will not have been all loss.[177]

[177] Carstens, C. C., "From the Ashes of Halifax," *Survey*, vol. xxxix, no. 13, p. 61.

CHAPTER IX

CONCLUSION

Recapitulation—The various steps in the study presented in propositional form—The rôle of catastrophe direct and indirect. (a) Directly prepares the ground-work for change by: (1) weakening social immobility; (2) producing fluidity of custom; (3) enhancing environal favorability for change—(b) Indirectly sets in motion factors determining the nature of the change such as: (1) the release of spirit and morale; (2) the play of imitation; (3) the stimulus of leaders and lookers-on; (4) the socialization of institutions.

If the preceding narrative has been successful in setting forth the facts as they were observed, the reader has now before him a fairly accurate picture of a community as it reacts under the stimulus of catastrophe and proceeds to adjust itself to the circumstantial pressure of new conditions. It will be well, however, for the sake of clearness in emphasizing our closing propositions to recapitulate one by one the various steps in our study. These steps while primarily intended to follow the natural order in point of time will also be seen to represent a definite sociological process of development.

At first the shock of the catastrophe was seen to have been sufficiently terrific to affect every inhabitant of the city. This fact gives peculiar value to the investigation. The more a shock is limited in extent the more its analysis grows in complexity. In such cases consideration must necessarily be given to the frontiers of influence. The chapter describing the shock also found the immediate reaction to have been a fairly general disintegration of social institutions, and of the usual methods of social control—in short, a dissolution of the customary. This turmoil into which society was thrown is sometimes called "fluidity," and, for lack of a better one, this term has been retained. It would thus appear that if it were later observed that essential social changes ensued, fluidity was one of the requisites of change; and this is indeed in perfect tally with previous thought upon the subject as set forth in our more theoretical introduction and expressed in the proposition that fluidity is fundamental to social change.

The more general and preliminary treatment over, individual and group reactions were then examined in greater detail, and the phenomena of the major sort were singled out and classified. These were found to be either abnormal and handicapping such as emotional parturition; or stimulative and promotive, as dynamogenic reaction. This constituted the material of the second chapter. Put in propositional form it would be that catastrophe is attended by phenomena of social psychology which may either retard or promote social reorganization.

Social organization came next in order, and because its progress was largely expedited by the organization of relief,—the first social activity,—the sociological factors observed in the latter have been recorded. These factors were classified as physical, including climate and topography, and psychological, such as leadership, suggestion, imitation, discussion, recognition of utility and consciousness of kind. Reference was also made to biological and equipmental considerations. Two conclusions of interest are here deducible: first, that part of society which is most closely organized and disciplined in normality first recovers social consciousness in catastrophe; second, it is only after division of function delegates to a special group the responsibility for relief work that public thought is directed to the resumption of a normal society. These conclusions emphasize the conservation value to society of a militia organization in every community and also of a permanent vigilance committee.

The fifth chapter introduced a relatively new element, the presence of which may be relied upon in all future emergencies, that of a disaster social service. Its contribution was that of skillful service and wise direction; its permanent effect, the socialization of the community. The value of the presence of visiting social specialists is in inverse proportion to the degree to which the socialization of a community has advanced. The practical conclusion is clearly that self-dependence of a community in adversity is furthered by the socialization of the existing institutions.

The next and latest group to function effectively was that of government, but social legislation when forth-coming, contributed an important and deciding influence, and was itself in turn enriched by the calamity. Brought to the test of comparison with observed facts the statement in the introduction receives abundant justification; namely, that catastrophe is in close association with progress in social legislation.

To the influences already mentioned an additional factor of recuperation is added,—the socio-economic one. Disaster-stricken communities cannot become normal until the social surplus is restored. They may however always count upon public aid. But there is found to be strongly suggested a correlation between the magnitude or striking character of a disaster and the generosity of the relief response.

The last chapter is devoted to a cataloging of the indications of social change from the standpoint of the community as a whole. The old social order is contrasted with that obtaining two years subsequent to the disaster. It here appeared that the city of Halifax had as a community undergone and is undergoing an extraordinary social change. This implies, according to the theory of social causation, an extraordinary antecedent. Before finally accepting the factor of catastrophe as such, the scientific reader may very properly ask whether there are not alternatives.

To this query the answer is that there are alternatives, other very considerable extra-social factors to be noted, but that catastrophe was itself the precipitating factor there is little room for doubt. Of the other factors two only are of sufficient weight for our present consideration. The earliest in order of time, and perhaps also in rank of importance is that which Halifax residents understand as the coming of the new ocean terminals. The coming was so sudden in the nature of its announcement, and meant for many so much depreciation in property values, that it had something of the nature of catastrophe within it. It altered very extensively the previously accepted ideas of residential and business and industrial sections of the city, and caused a jolt in the body politic, such as had not visited it for years—not since the middle of the nineteenth century brought the revolutionizing steam. It is not to be denied that this factor has contributed not a little to the weakening of immobility, and the preparation of the ground for an inrush of the spirit of progress.

The other factor was the war. The war functioned mightily in community organization for service. It brought prosperity to many a door, and whetted the appetite of many a merchant to put the business of peace on a war basis. But it would be merely speculation to say that prosperity would have continued in peace. Indeed such a conclusion would not be historically justifiable. Halifax has been through three important wars. In each, "trade was active, prices were high, the population increased, industry was stimulated by the demand, rents doubled and trebled, streets were uncommonly busy." But in each case also Halifax settled back to her ante-bellum sluggishness. In 1816 Halifax began to feel the reaction consequent upon the close of a war. The large navy and army were withdrawn and Halifax and its inhabitants "bore the appearance of a town at the close of a fair. The sudden change from universal hustle and business to ordinary pursuits made this alteration at times very perceptible. Money gradually disappeared and the failure of several mercantile establishments added to the general distress." But the closing of the war, now a hundred years later, has exhibited no such relapse. On the other hand Halifax grows daily more prosperous and progressive than before. Her bank clearings do not fail, but rather increase. There is clearly some further influence associated with this change.

But there is a very real sense in which the war may indeed be said to have been the factor,—if we mean by it the fact that through the war and as a direct result of war-service the city was laid half in ruins by possibly the greatest single catastrophe on the American Continent. If we mean this, we have named the all-precipitating and determining event. The catastrophe was an episode of the great war.

It only remains to add by way of clearer definition that the rôle of catastrophe appears to be both direct and indirect. Functioning directly, it prepares the ground-work for social change by (1) weakening social immobility; (2) precipitating fluidity of custom; (3) forcing environal favorability for change. Indirectly, it sets in motion factors determining the nature of the social change, such as (1) the release of spirit and morale; (2) the play of imitation; (3) the stimulus of leaders and lookers-on; (4) the socialization of institutions.

Our final principle[178] thus appears to be that progress in catastrophe is a re-

[178] The two additional propositions suggested in the Introduction, namely, that the degree of fluidity seems to vary directly as the shock of the catastrophe, and that brusk

sultant of specific conditioning factors some of which are subject to social control. If there is one thing more than another which we would emphasize in conclusion it is this final principle. Progress is not necessarily a natural or assured result of change. It comes only as a result of effort that is wisely expended and sacrifice which is sacrifice in truth.

That the nature of the social change in Halifax is one in the direction of progress we think to be based on reason and not alone on hope. That it is also our fervent hope, we need hardly add. But every Haligonian who cherishes for his city the vision which this book contains, may help mightily to bring it to pass by making effort his watchword and intelligence his guide. We do not say it will all come tomorrow. We do say a wonderful beginning has been made since yesterday. And this is bright for the future. In no better words can we conclude than in those of one of her greatest lovers: "Changes must come to Halifax. This is a world of change. But every true Haligonian hopes that the changes will not disfigure his beloved city, but only heighten and enhance the intimate and haunting charms she borrows from the sea."[179]

revolution in the conditions of life accomplish not sudden, but gradual changes in society, require a study of comparative catastrophic phenomena for verification or rejection.

[179] MacMechan, *op. cit.*, p. 336.

VITA

Born at Hammond River, Province of New Brunswick, Canada. Son of Samuel I. and Mary E. Perkins Prince. Graduate of St. John (N. B.) High School, the University of Toronto, Wycliffe College (Tor.). Taught at Ridley College, St. Catharines, Ont. Appointed to staff of St. Paul's Halifax N. S. Studied for doctorate at Columbia University. Subject of primary interest, Sociology; of secondary interest, Statistics and Social Legislation. Graduate courses with Professors, Giddings, Tenney, Chaddock, Lindsay, Andrews, Montague, McCrea. President of the British Empire Club of the University.

INDEX

A

Administration of relief *12, 38*
Ameliorative legislation *46*
Analytic psychology *15*
Anger *12*
Anxiety *9*
Army *35, 36*
Association *34, 41*
Attention *xvi, xviii, 18, 24, 31, 37, 41, 55, 67*
Authority *36, 52, 65, 70*

B

Behavior *xvi, 14, 15, 17*
Beliefs *9, 58*
Bereavement *14*
Body politic *xviii, 12, 21, 27, 74*

C

Capital *70*
Cataclysm *xv*
Catastrophe and progress *xiv*
Catastrophe and Social Change *57*
Catastrophe and Social Disintegration *1*
Catastrophe and Social Economy *34*
Catastrophe and Social Legislation *46*
Catastrophe and Social Organization *21*
Catastrophe and Social Psychology *7*
Catastrophe and Social Surplus *53*
Ceremony *58*
Charity *xix, 44*
Child welfare *67*
Churches *2, 5, 30, 31, 43, 49, 58, 70*
Circumstantial pressure *6, 21, 24, 31, 72*
Civic authority *47, 48*
Civic improvement *65*

Civilization *4, 15, 34*
Clergy *30, 36*
Clinics *67, 68*
Clubs *60*
Collective behavior *21, 25*
Commerce *xviii, 57, 59, 68*
Commercialized recreation *69*
Communication *19, 21, 22, 28*
Community *vi, xvii, xviii, xix, 5, 6, 7, 15, 18, 19, 20, 21, 23, 25, 26, 27, 28, 30, 32, 33, 34, 35, 36, 37, 38, 39, 41, 42, 43, 44, 45, 46, 49, 50, 51, 53, 55, 56, 57, 58, 59, 64, 65, 66, 68, 69, 70, 72, 73, 74*
Comparative catastrophe *55*
Compensation *43, 44, 50*
Component groups *28*
Consciousness *8, 11, 21, 23, 26, 61, 73*
Contagion of feeling *11*
Conventionality *7, 15*
Coöperation *vi, 36, 38, 41, 69, 70*
Courts *43, 49*
Crisis and catastrophe *xvi*
Criticism *36, 41, 42, 44*
Crowd *7, 9, 10, 11, 12, 13, 41, 55*
Culture *xviii, xix, 34*
Curiosity *12*
Custom *xv, xvii, xviii, 7, 15, 23, 26, 27, 72, 74*
Cycles *xv*

D

Death rate *67*
Degree of progress *xix*
Delinquency *69*
Delusion *7, 9*
Determination *12, 20, 61*
Disaster *vi, xix, 4, 23, 37, 39, 41, 50, 53, 73*
Discussion *8, 15, 19, 21, 24, 26, 28, 67, 73*
Disease *xix, 8, 67, 68*
Disorganization of business *4, 21*
Dispensary *34, 39, 66*
Diverse phenomena *7*
Diversity of capacity *27*
Division of labor *27*
Dynamic forces *xvii*
Dynamogenic reactions *20*

E

Economic vigor *28*
Education *xviii, 26, 36, 39, 46, 57, 65, 68, 69, 70*
Educational institutions *68*
Educational psychology *69*
Educational sociology *69*
Emergency *vi, 17, 19, 22, 30, 33, 35, 36, 37, 38, 45, 48*
Emotion *xvii, 7, 8, 12, 13, 14, 17*
Endurance *17, 18, 21*
Energies *17, 27*
Envy *12, 57*
Erroneous recognition *9*
Evolution *xiv, xv, 19, 46*
Exaltation *13*
Expansion of business *57*
Expectancy *xv, 11*

F

Factors in social change *xiv, xv*
Family *4, 19, 22, 30, 37, 38, 39, 43, 70*
Fatigue *7, 13, 17, 18, 35*
Fear *4, 9, 11, 12, 17, 23*
Feelings of security *10*
First aid *10, 22*
Fluidity *xvii, xviii, xix, 6, 72, 74*
Flux *xvii, 6*
Food-getting *9*
Fraternal societies *44*

G

Generosity *18, 19, 20, 53, 55, 73*
Geographic determinants *21*
Government *xiv, xviii, 4, 23, 40, 42, 45, 46, 47, 48, 49, 50, 52, 56, 58, 66, 67, 69, 73*
Gratitude *xx, 12*
Great man *45*
Greed *12, 17*
Gregarious instinct *9, 10, 23, 26*
Grief *8, 9, 14, 41*
Group *vi, xv, xvi, 10, 19, 21, 27, 33, 46, 53, 72, 73*

H

Habit *xvi, xviii, 17, 27*
Habitation *9, 23*
Hallucination *7, 8, 9*

Happiness *28, 54, 65*
Heredity *17, 26*
Heroism *7, 18, 19*
History *vi, xiii, xiv, xv, 2, 11, 55, 57, 58, 59, 61*
Homes *1, 2, 5, 11, 14, 15, 22, 23, 32, 40, 57, 58, 66*
Homogeneity *27*
Hospitals *14, 17, 23, 25, 38, 39, 40*
Housing *57, 65, 66, 69, 71*
Human nature *7, 42*
Hyper-suggestibility *12*
Hypnosis *13*

I

Ideals of legislation *46*
Imagination *xvii, 4, 13, 55*
Imitation *xv, 21, 23, 26, 27, 32, 72, 73, 74*
Impulsive social action *11*
Indications of change *57, 60*
Indications of social change *73*
Indices of business *61*
Industrial accidents *51*
Industrial fatigue *69*
Industrial hygiene *68*
Industry *4, 27, 57, 59, 74*
Instinct of pugnacity *9, 10*
Instincts *xvii, xviii, 7, 9, 10, 11, 12*

J

Jealousy *12*
Justice *xviii, 38, 42*
Juvenile delinquency *69*

K

Kindliness *13, 18*

L

Labor *xx, 16, 27, 46, 50, 59, 70*
Law *5, 7, 15, 16, 20, 26, 27, 32, 42, 51, 58, 59, 66*
Leadership *15, 21, 22, 26, 36, 45, 47, 48, 56, 66, 73*
Legislation *xx, 46, 50, 51, 52, 56, 66*
Like-mindedness *27*
Like response *10*

M

Magic *xviii, 32*
Maternity *14, 67*
Medical inspection *68*
Medical relief *35, 68*
Medical Social Service *38, 39, 40, 45, 70*
Men skilled in dealing with crises *34*
Mental hygiene *67*
Mental unity *10*
Ministerial Association *70*
Models *xix, 20, 32*
Modes of affective experience *12*
Morale *xix, 49, 50, 72, 74*
Mores *xvii, xviii, 27*
Morgue service *45*
Mortality *67, 69*
Mutual Aid *7, 18, 19, 20*

N

Navy *4, 57, 74*
Normality *26, 28, 73*

O

Oneiric delirium *13*
Organization *xix, 21, 24, 25, 26, 27, 35, 36, 37, 39, 41, 42, 44, 45, 47, 66, 67, 68, 69, 70, 73, 74*
Organization of relief *21, 27, 73*
Orientation *60*
Original tendencies *9*
Over-emphasis of government *xviii, 58*

P

Pain *5, 7, 13, 14, 17, 18, 54*
Parental instinct *9, 10*
Pensions *40*
Percentage of indifference *64*
Percentage of Interest *64*
Personal crises *xvii*
Phenomena *vi, 5, 6, 7, 10, 12, 14, 15, 17, 20, 72, 73, 75*
Philanthropy *17*
Physiological reactions *7*
Pity *9*
Pluralistic behavior *xvii*
Plural leadership *15*

Police *15, 20, 31, 47, 48*
Policy of centralization *36*
Political Action *57, 64*
Political Science *47, 50*
Poor laws *46*
Population *xviii, 25, 26, 53, 54, 57, 59, 63, 64, 69, 74*
Post-catastrophic phenomena *7, 15*
Power to meet crises *34*
Precipitating agent *xv*
Preparedness *24*
Press *41, 70*
Primitive household *27*
Principle of Indemnity *43*
Principle of Restitution *43*
Principles of Relief *34, 35, 36, 43, 55*
Procedure *xx, 33, 42, 47, 51*
Production *xviii, 29*
Progress in catastrophe *xix, 74*
Progress in legislation *46*
Progress in social legislation *50, 52, 73*
Protocracy *21, 22, 27*
Psychology of helpfulness *19, 37*
Psychology of Insanity *8, 14*
Public Health *39, 51, 66, 67, 68*
Public Opinion *37, 42, 49, 51, 61*
Public Safety *10, 34, 35*
Public Utilities *28*

R

Reconditioning of instincts *xvi*
Recreation *xviii, 46, 57, 65, 69, 70*
Regional influence *25*
Rehabilitation *vi, 34, 36, 37, 38, 39, 40, 41, 42, 43, 45, 48, 49*
Relief organization *36, 38, 48*
Religion *xvi, 57, 58*
Repression *7, 15, 16*
Reproductive system of society *4*
Resentment *12, 15*
Residuum of relief *44*
Resistance to change *xviii*
Responsiveness to rumor *12*
Restitution *42, 43, 44*
Resumption of normal society *33*
Retrogressive evolution *xv*
Revolution *xvi, xvii, xix, 11, 75*
Ritual *xviii*

Rumor *15, 23*

S

Sabbath observance *32*
Sanitation *25, 51*
Schools *vii, 2, 15, 30, 31, 43, 49, 67, 68*
Science *xviii, 5, 6, 39, 53, 63*
Security *xviii*
Self-preservation *10*
Sensation *7*
Shibboleths *32*
Shock reaction *7*
Significance of crisis *xvi*
Social action *24*
Social age *70*
Social aggregation *23*
Social causation *73*
Social change *vi, xiv, xv, xvi, xvii, xviii, xix, 6, 56, 58, 72, 73, 74, 75*
Social classes *44*
Social consciousness *22, 73*
Social conservation *27, 33, 36*
Social contrasts *5*
Social control *xviii, xix, 6, 72, 75*
Social Economy *vi, 33, 45*
Social effects *xv, 10, 31*
Social factors *45, 74*
Social immobility *57, 58, 72, 74*
Social institutions *xvi, 6, 72*
Social insurance *70*
Socialization *17, 37, 44, 72, 73, 74*
Socialized recreation *69, 70*
Social legislation *vi, xx, 46, 49, 50, 51, 52, 73, 76*
social memory *xx, 19*
Social mind *28*
Social order *1, 25, 27, 73*
Social organization *vi, 7, 20, 21, 22, 26, 27, 47, 73*
social policy *34, 69*
Social pressure *21, 23, 32*
Social psychology *6, 7, 10, 15, 20, 73*
Social relief *45*
Social reorganization *25, 73*
Social self-control *27*
Social sensorium *21*
Social Service *34, 35, 36, 41, 42, 45, 56, 70, 73*
Social specialists *27, 35, 73*
Social Surplus *26, 53, 54, 73*

Societies *xviii, 45, 70*
Society *xv, xvii, xviii, xix, 5, 6, 7, 8, 13, 15, 19, 22, 26, 27, 28, 31, 34, 39, 41, 44, 46, 58, 68, 69, 72, 73, 75*
Sociological factors *21, 26, 73*
Sociology *vi, xv, xvii, xix, xx, 4, 6, 7, 11, 22, 25, 43, 51, 56, 58, 59, 76*
Sorrow *5, 13, 14*
State *xvii, xviii, xx, 5, 6, 12, 14, 34, 35, 42, 47, 51, 53*
State and voluntary associations *27*
Statistics *76*
Stimulus *xvi, xix, 6, 12, 17, 18, 32, 72, 74*
Stimulus of lookers-on *27, 32*
Sub-normal *68*
Suggestibility *11, 15*
Suicide *14*
Supervised playgrounds *68*
Survival *19*
Sympathy *6, 13, 14, 20, 50, 55*

T

Taboo *15*
Themistes *xvii*
Topography *25, 26, 73*
Transportation *4, 21, 22, 35*

U

Under-nutrition *54*
Unemployment *21, 61*
Utility *52, 65, 73*
Utility of association *21, 22, 26*

V

Vicissitudes *xiv, xv, 42*
Vigilance committee *33, 73*
Virgin fields in Sociology *xiv*
Vital statistics *68*
Volition *18, 24*

W

War *xiv, 1, 2, 3, 8, 11, 13, 15, 31, 32, 42, 44, 50, 52, 53, 56, 61, 62, 69, 74*
Wealth *53, 58*
Welfare *34, 38, 39, 65, 66*
Welfare Bureau *vii*
Will *17, 44*
Workmen's Compensation *49*

Worship *xviii*

Z

Zeal *12*

Lector House believes that a society develops through a two-fold approach of continuous learning and adaptation, which is derived from the study of classic literary works spread across the historic timeline of literature records. Therefore, we aim at reviving, repairing and redeveloping all those inaccessible or damaged but historically as well as culturally important literature across subjects so that the future generations may have an opportunity to study and learn from past works to embark upon a journey of creating a better future.

This book is a result of an effort made by Lector House towards making a contribution to the preservation and repair of original ancient works which might hold historical significance to the approach of continuous learning across subjects.

HAPPY READING & LEARNING!

LECTOR HOUSE
LECTOR HOUSE LLP
E-MAIL: lectorpublishing@gmail.com

9 789356 146549

Printed by Libri Plureos GmbH in Hamburg,
Germany

9 789356 146549